THE GREEN MACHINE

THE STORY OF EDINBURGH UNIVERSITY

HARE AND HOUNDS 1960-1970

To DAVID

Fellow Athlete!

All best,

Alistair

Alistair Blamire

Printed by

Leiston Press Ltd

Masterlord Industrial Estate

Leiston

Suffolk

IP16 4JD

Telephone Number: 01728 833003

Email: glenn@leistonpress.com

Web: www.leistonpress.com

Published by ELS Press, 2017

ISBN 978-1-911311-25-6

To those who 'also ran',

without whom there would never be a winner,

and to the unsung officials,

without whom there would never be a race

The Author was a member of Edinburgh University Hare and Hounds from 1964 to 1971, and Captain in 1966 - 67. He was a British International on the track in 1969 and ran for Scotland in the International Cross Country Championships on several occasions. He retired from competitive athletics in the late 1970s and still runs four times a week, when pulled muscles and stiff joints permit.

AUTHOR'S NOTE:

This story is primarily a factual and objective account but, because I make up a small part of it, I hesitated over whether it should be written in the first person or the third person. There are long tracts where this is not an issue but, after much deliberation, and a fair amount of consultation, I decided that it was more appropriate to use the first person whenever I appear in the narrative, regardless of how isolated the reference is within the text.

CONTENTS

FOREWORD

Quite a number of running clubs have produced club histories. Among those with which I am familiar are Thames Hare and Hounds (founded in 1875), Shettleston Harriers and Edinburgh Southern Harriers. I am sure there are many more. This new history of the Edinburgh University Hare and Hounds team of the 1960s therefore fills a gap.

Edinburgh University Hare and Hounds has long been one of the leading cross country clubs in Scotland. In the 1960s it ventured south to London (winning the Hyde Park Relay three times and the British Universities Cross Country Championships) and quite a few members achieved international success, in two cases - Fergus Murray and Gareth Bryan-Jones - even competing in the Olympic Games. The team had many victories in club, university and national competition and between them Fergus Murray and Andy McKean alone won seven individual Scottish National Cross Country titles in their running careers.

Although the club's huge successes were in the 1960s, an earlier champion was Yorkshireman Adrian Jackson, who ran three times in the International Cross Country Championships. A further ten members of Edinburgh University Hare and Hounds team of the period reached this level in cross country, and the club was also represented at the Commonwealth Games and on the road and track for Great Britain.

The 'spiritual home' of the club in the 1960s, as it were, was 'The Zoo', a large rented house in Morningside Drive in Edinburgh, whose residents, and occasional visitors such as myself, aimed to achieve one hundred miles a week in training. It was called 'The Zoo' in recognition of the nicknames of the runners: 'The Beast' (Fergus Murray), 'The Bear' (Chris Elson) and 'The Crab' (Martin Craven). These names are explained in this book.

In a country besotted with football – a sport that Scotland has not been particularly good at recently – the Edinburgh University Hare and Hounds team deserves considerably more recognition than it has received. Many of its runners achieved much but remained likeable and modest. The club embodies the spirit of Charles Hamilton Sorley's *'Ungirt Runners'* of the early twentieth century:

"The rain is on our lips, we do not run for prize
But the storm the water whips and the wave howls to the skies.
The winds arise and strike it and scatter it like sand,
And we run because we like it through the broad bright land"

This is an excellent production: buy it.

Donald Macgregor

St Andrews, April 2017

1

INTRODUCTION

At the Scottish Cross Country Union Championships at Hamilton Racecourse in 1967 a team of students from Edinburgh University Hare and Hounds placed their six counting runners in the first 28 finishers in a field of over 300 in the Senior event. Their winning margin of 144 points was the highest in the 70 year history of the event, and has only been exceeded once since then, over 50 years later. Even more extraordinary is the fact that the Edinburgh University Junior team also won their team race on the same day, further contributing to a remarkable achievement for a university sport in which most participants have graduated and left by the age of 22.

But these are only two small, little-known statistics in the story of this outstanding cross country team which dominated long distance running in Scotland during the 1960s, when many team and individual achievements were recorded over a period of unusual longevity for such a successful university sports team. In addition to the 'Scottish', in which they were senior winners in 1966, 1967 and 1968, they won the prestigious Hyde Park Relay three years in a row, breaking the course record on each occasion, many District and University Championships and, most significantly of all, the British Universities Cross Country Championships at Parliament Hill Fields in London in February 1967. At the Scottish Universities Cross Country Championships in Aberdeen in 1966, the green-vested Edinburgh team packed their eight runners in the first nine finishers in the first team race and had the first eight finishers in the second team race. Individually, runners represented Scotland, Northern Ireland, Wales and Great Britain, Scottish Universities and British Universities at cross country and set numerous records on the track and on the roads.

The inspiration behind the successes of Edinburgh University Hare and Hounds at this time was Fergus Murray from Dundee who studied chemistry at Edinburgh from 1961 to 1966. Murray, of the prodigious training schedules and Spartan lifestyle, represented Great Britain at the 1964 Olympic Games and both Great Britain and Scotland on many other occasions. His training, based on the philosophies of the eccentric Australian coach Percy Cerutty and his New Zealand counterpart Arthur Lydiard, inspired many young athletes in Scotland at the time and went a long way to explaining the successes of the Edinburgh team, even long after Murray had left for a post graduate diploma at Oxford University in 1966.

However, this doesn't account for the diverse backgrounds of the top runners in the team at this time, what motivated them to take up running in the first place, and what sustained them during long hours of training. Murray's example was clearly a major factor once individual runners joined the Hare and Hounds (and, in some cases, beforehand too) but the team's success thereafter was often the result of individual rivalry as well as team spirit.

Runners were inspired by the great British distance runners of the time, such as Murray, and motivated by a desire for success, and perhaps recognition, as well as camaraderie and the sheer enjoyment of the sport itself. There was no formal tuition, only constant reference to the coaching methods of the great gurus of the period, Lydiard, Cerutty and Franz Stampfl. Lydiard's mantra of 100 miles a week, although not espoused by everyone in the team, was a target for some and a constant reference point for others, week after week. They knew little about the physiology of running – it was all about what you heard, what you read and shared with others, how hard it was, how you felt.

There was no discussion about diet, no heart monitors, oxygen tents or treadmills, no lottery funding or easy global communication to share training methods and advice on supplements and, more often than not, little restraint once the race was over and the pub doors opened. It was reminiscent of the approach of the fictional Alf Tupper, the 'Tough of the Track', athletics hero from the pages of 'The Rover' and 'The Victor' comics, who could run a four minute mile after a fish supper and a sleepless night in the railway sidings: an interesting working class counterpoint to the 'effortless superiority' of the gentlemen amateur athletes of Oxford and Cambridge in the immediate post-war period.

This account is not intended to be a moral crusade or just a *résumé* of the achievements of one unusually successful group of athletes but rather to find out how and why it all happened when it did – what made these runners tick, how they were motivated and inspired, and how they coped with pressure, discomfort, failure and success. Perhaps it may inspire the ambitious young runners of today to recognise that success in athletics can be achieved without necessarily adopting the props and paraphernalia of modern mass participation and that, notwithstanding the achievements of the great professional runners of the current era, a high level of success is possible, without compromising one's lifestyle too much, through dedication, ambition, team spirit, a focussed training programme, and perhaps a little talent thrown in.

Chapter One

TRAINING METHODS AND THE AMATEUR ETHOS

In order to understand the circumstances confronting the Edinburgh University Hare and Hounds team in the 1960s it is necessary, in the first instance, to take a step back and to review the main issues in terms of the evolution of coaching and training, and the amateur ethos which pervaded the sport of athletics at the time.

* * *

Despite the successes of athletes such as Olympic champions Douglas Lowe and Tommy Hampson, and world mile and half mile record holder Sydney Wooderson, in the 1920s and 30s, Britain was a relative backwater of organised distance running training in the years immediately after World War Two. There was a lingering attitude among the ruling classes that it was somehow vulgar to take sport, and training in particular, too seriously. Sport was to be a strictly amateur pastime far removed from the seedy world of boxing or the unseemly mass popularity of professional football.

This manifested itself in events like the annual Gentlemen versus Players cricket match which was played as recently as 1962, and in the antipathy in rugby, now a mutual if wary respect, between the amateurs of Rugby Union, which was a sport developed through the public schools, and professional Rugby League, which had its roots in the industrial north of England. But the divide was most apparent in track and field athletics, primarily through the huge influence of the modern Olympic Games which first took place in 1896. This was the event which athletes the world over would give their eye teeth to compete in but it remained strictly amateur, maintaining the importance, in theory at least, 'not of the winning, but of the taking part'[1]. Any suggestion of monetary gain through sport would result in athletes being banned from amateur competition, and consequently from competing in the Olympic Games.

Sporting history is littered with examples of athletes being deprived of the opportunity of Olympic success because of seemingly minor transgressions involving payments. Even great runners like Paavo Nurmi

---

[1] This quote is attributed to Pierre de Coubertin, the founder of the International Olympic Committee and the alleged 'father' of the modern Olympic movement. There is a school of thought that his commitment to the amateur ethos gave the upper classes greater control over athletic competition.

and Gunder Hägg, no doubt aware of their 'box office appeal' during their prime, fell foul of the rules. The English distance runner John Tarrant could not compete officially in amateur events for many years, and was unable to represent his country, despite being the best ultra long distance runner of his time, because he had received a few pounds in prize money as a teenage boxer.

As levels of training became more and more intense, nations would look to ways of circumventing the amateur code in order to gain advantage over their opponents. In the Soviet Union and other Eastern European countries, promising athletes were recruited into the armed forces where a systematic programme of training could be undertaken behind the façade of a military career. Meanwhile, in the United States, the collegiate system provided similar opportunities for athletes to train on a near full-time basis. Over time commercial pressures in track and field athletics became too great and the Olympic Games eventually became fully open to professionalism from 1988.

In Britain, a parallel world of professional athletics or 'pedestrianism', in which athletes competed openly for money, carried on in its own traditional way through events such as Highland Games and Miners' Galas. At the renowned Powderhall Meeting on New Year's Day in Edinburgh, athletes such as the sprinter George McNeill and the Bathgate middle distance runner Michael Glen were capable of performances at least as impressive as, if not better than, the top amateurs of their day. This was a much more arcane area of the sport with specific traditions both in terms of training regimes and competition and it continues in this form to the present day, despite the sport as a whole becoming open in the 1980s.

In 1972 Michael O'Hara, an American basketball and ice hockey entrepreneur, formed the International Track Association, a travelling circus of former amateur stars who competed, on a professional basis, in a series of track and field events all over Europe and the US. However, the ITA failed to catch on and eventually went bankrupt in 1976, primarily because at that time athletes did not want to lose their amateur status, and therefore the opportunity to compete in major Games. Payments were often, in any case, less than the top athletes could earn 'under the counter' on the amateur circuit.

In the amateur area of the sport, attitudes to training began to change in the early 1950s in Britain as the influence of distance running programmes developed in Germany, Scandinavia and other European countries began to take hold. Before that training was largely experimental with little scientific basis and some eccentric approaches in preparing for competition. Much of the training undergone would be considered a waste of time today, other than improving general fitness and providing the psychological benefit of confidence building. The 40 mile Sunday walks undertaken by Dunky Wright in the 1930s as part of his long distance training, for example, would have had very little aerobic benefit despite Wright's stellar career as a runner, including a close fourth place in the 1932 Olympic Games marathon in Los Angeles.

INTERVAL RUNNING

Modern training techniques in long distance running had developed in Europe between the wars following on from the Finns, who dominated the sport after World War One, and in particular Paavo Nurmi, who was one of the first great athletes to consider all aspects of training from diet and rest to different forms of exercise. In the 1930s, the German coach Woldemar Gerschler, working with a cardiologist, Dr Herbert Reindel, started to experiment with the interval running first dabbled in by Nurmi, establishing in particular the importance of the recovery periods between repetitions.

Gerschler's model involved fast runs of between 100 metres and 400 metres at sufficient pace to achieve a pulse rate of 180 beats per minute. The length of the rest period between the fast runs was dependent on the heart rate reducing to 120 beats per minute. The training benefit came with a lowered heart rate which allowed a greater quantity of blood to be pumped at each beat. The maximum length of the rest period was calculated at 90 seconds and if the heart rate of 120 beats per minute could not be achieved within this period, the heart was considered overworked, resulting in excessive fatigue, with diminishing benefit. Conversely, if the rate of 120 could be achieved more quickly, the rest interval could be reduced accordingly. The main purpose was that the repetitions were run at the same speed with the length of the intervals between being the critical training principle.

However, this scientific approach was difficult to monitor, especially if runners were training on their own, although it could be emulated in an experiential way by dedicated athletes who realised that too much recovery between efforts was too easy. In simple terms, an example of this would be a session consisting of 12 x 200 metres with 200 metres jog in between (too long a recovery) compared with 12 x 300 metres with 100 metres jog. With the latter programme, the same overall distance was covered, but with greater cardiovascular benefit.

In 1939, Gerschler's protégé Rudolf Harbig vindicated his coaching methods by lowering the world record for the 800 metres by 1.8 seconds on a 500 metre track[2] in Milan, outkicking the pace setter, his great rival Mario Lanzi of Italy, in the finishing straight with a time of 1 minute 46.6 seconds. This equated to a margin of approximately 15 metres faster than anyone had achieved before[3] and the record stood for 16 years until it was surpassed by Roger Moens of Belgium at Bislett Stadium in Oslo in August 1955. But Harbig, despite his celebrity, was not exempt from total commitment to the German war effort. He was sent to the Eastern Front, serving as a sergeant in Göring's elite paratroop regiment, and went missing, presumed killed in action, in Ukraine in March 1944.

Gerschler continued his work after the war, his most significant achievement being the unexpected Olympic 1,500 metres victory in 1952 of Josy Barthel of Luxembourg. Although Barthel is often regarded as a little known prodigy of the time, in fact he was a finalist in the 1,500 metres at the 1948 Olympics, finishing 10th, and won three titles at the World Student Games in 1949 and 1951. Sadly, Barthel's success was tainted later on by unproven but credible allegations of drug taking, which was not subject at that time to any of the scrutiny and controversy it attracts today. The 'medication' was reputedly administered by Gerschler and Reindel as part of Barthel's training programme, a precursor of the questionable methods of some coaches and athletes in more recent years.

However, the greatest exponent of interval running was the inspirational and charismatic Czech Emil Zatopek, winner of three gold medals in the 1952 Olympic Games. Zatopek was mainly self-coached and undertook prodigious training sessions such as 80 x 400 metres which was the equivalent, including the 150 metre jog between each repetition, of 28 miles run as an interval session. He could maintain this astonishing level of training for as much as ten days in a row. He set a total of 18 world records

---

[2] 500m tracks were more common on the continent at that time as they related more directly to the standard metric distances of 1,500m, 5,000m and 10,000m. 500m and 1,000m events were also held on a more regular basis. In Britain, tracks became standardised at 440 yards (later 400m), or four laps to the mile, resulting in 200m, 400m and 800m becoming accepted international distances. 400m probably also prevailed as the standard track size for outdoor competition because it could be fitted conveniently round a football or rugby pitch, especially after the recent introduction of retractable seating which allows spectators to be closer to the action regardless of the sport.

[3] The previous record, set in 1938, was held by Sydney Wooderson at 1 minute 48.4 seconds.

over the period between 1949 and 1955, leading an extraordinary life in a land besieged by the conflicting ideologies of neighbouring regimes before, during and after World War Two[4]. Interestingly, Zatopek never really succeeded as a coach himself, apparently because his athletes were unable to cope with the intense levels of training he demanded of them.

In Scotland, Ian Binnie was a relative pioneer who followed Zatopek's example in the 1950s with training sessions which included 40 x 300 metres with 100 metres jog between. Like almost all of his contemporaries, a self-coached athlete, Binnie set numerous Scottish distance records between 1953 and 1957, and narrowly failed to break the world record for the one hour run at Cowal Highland Gathering in Dunoon in 1953. As an interesting aside most of Binnie's records were set in Scotland and, although he was invited to represent Great Britain, an offer he chose to decline, his reputation never really reached southern radar.

Interval running was also the forte of the Austrian coach Franz Stampfl whose methods inspired Roger Bannister to run the first sub-four minute mile in 1954. In contrast to the extremes practised by athletes such as Zatopek and Binnie, this form of training could also be a very effective way of gaining fitness quickly, and intensive sessions could be over in as little as 20 minutes. It seemed an ideal way of gaining fitness without the stigma of being overcommitted to training and became a preserve of the Oxbridge athletes of the 1950s who allegedly regarded excessive physical exercise as a rather unseemly pursuit. In Bannister's words, they were haunted 'by the fear of being thought to take anything too seriously'. However, Bannister was much more than a dilettante who floated through life on a wave of exceptional natural talent. As a serious medical student he questioned the methods of his original coach, Bill Thomas, who had advised the 1936 Olympic Champion Jack Lovelock and was still in charge of coaching at Oxford University when Bannister was a student. Thomas seemed to rely on intuition which, particularly as he was a non-runner himself, did not go down well with Bannister's enquiring, scientific mind.

The attitude of the Corinthian amateurs of Oxbridge reputedly resulted

---

[4] Many accounts of Zatopek's life and running career have been written, not least the three books published in 2016, 'Today We Die a Little: The Rise and Fall of Emil Zatopek, Olympic Legend' by Richard Askwith, 'Endurance: The Extraordinary Life and Times of Emil Zatopek' by Rick Broadbent and 'Quicksilver: The Mercurial Emil Zatopek' by Pat Butcher.

in Bannister failing to win the Olympic 1,500 metres in Helsinki in 1952, because his lack of aerobic background fitness was unable to sustain him through the three rounds, on successive days, of a championship event. The 1,500 metres event at these Games was originally intended to be competed for by way of heats and a final but an additional semi-final round was added for the first time due to the unexpectedly large number of competitors. Bannister finished fourth in the final.

In truth, Bannister was an extremely gifted amateur who found the pressure of expectation in Britain, egged on by a critical and demanding press, too much to live up to at the Games. Chris Chataway, another hugely talented athlete from Oxford with a similar training background, led the great triumvirate of Zatopek, Schade and Mimoun into the final bend of the 5,000 metres at the same Games only to lose his balance, trip on the kerb and fall, only 120 yards from the finishing line. He eventually finishing a distant fifth in the same time as Gordon Pirie who had been dropped by the leaders several laps from home. The estimable Chataway came to regret his approach to training in his later years, expressing huge admiration for the 'intelligent' attitude of the likes of Zatopek and Bannister's great rival, the Australian miler John Landy[5].

The overriding problem with interval running was that fitness levels could quickly be dissipated and it was only really effective in the longer term when combined with equally serious aerobic training. Pirie, who despised the attitude of the gifted amateur, trained under the influence of the European coaches of the day and followed the Zatopek dictum of gruelling training sessions. As an amateur athlete Pirie was far ahead of his time in seeking out Gerschler in Germany and working with him on programmed interval running.

Sadly, although Pirie's best times bear witness to the benefits of intensive training, he failed to succeed in championships other than gaining a consolatory silver in the 1956 Olympic 5,000 metres in Melbourne, after his epic battle against the relentless front running of the Soviet Vladimir Kuts, five days earlier in the 10,000 metres, and a bronze medal at 5,000 metres in the European Championships in 1958. However, Pirie's defining world record of 13 minutes 36.8 seconds for this event, set in Bergen, Norway in June 1956, was so far ahead of its time in British terms that it would have ranked him as high as seventh in the UK rankings even 60 years later.

---

[5] See '3:59.4, The Quest to Break the 4 Minute Mile' by John Bryant, page 296.

FARTLEK

During the years of World War Two neutral Sweden, anxious to reverse its embarrassing cross country defeats to the Finns in the 1920s and 30s, had become an isolated centre for distance running with the development of *fartlek* (or 'speed play') by Gösta Holmér, winner of a bronze medal in the 1912 Olympic decathlon, from the late 1930s. This method of training gave athletes another simple yet balanced formula to develop aerobic and anaerobic fitness levels, combining longer runs with a more free spirited form of interval efforts. The most important attribute of *fartlek* was that it avoided interval training on the track which could lead to boredom and mental staleness due to its relentless repetitiveness.

The romantic notion was of *fartlek* in a Swedish summer consisting of runs through the pine forests and along the edges of the lakes. In more specific terms it involved running at speed over distances varying from 100 to 1,000 metres, alternating with jogging, ideally over shorter distances, in between. Despite Gerschler's dismissive attitude that it was not exact enough in scientific terms, it could be very intensive too, but pleasantly varied, and it led to the phenomenal successes of Gunder Hägg and Arne Andersson, who between them lowered the world mile record by 5 seconds in the space of three years in the 1940s.

When Hägg set his first world mile record of 4 minutes 6.2 seconds in 1942 he had barely been near a running track for over a year and, although he and Andersson failed in their bid to achieve the 'Holy Grail' of the four minute mile, Hägg nevertheless had the consolation of becoming the first man to break 14 minutes for 5,000 metres in September 1942. His time of 13 minutes 58.2 seconds stood as the world record for 12 years. However, we will never know whether Hägg and Andersson would have been as dominant, or indeed been pushed below the four minute barrier for the mile, if they had had more competition at that time.

Like interval running, *fartlek* endures to the present day as a very important component of a balanced training programme.

CERUTTY

After World War Two, while Gerschler was pursuing his scientific approach to interval training, the idiosyncratic Australian coach Percy Wells Cerutty developed his own version of *fartlek* at his seaside training camp at Portsea in Victoria. Cerutty had not been a successful athlete himself, primarily due to ill health, but he was driven by an intense desire to fulfil his athletic potential at whatever level he could achieve in the circumstances. This attitude dictated the development of his philosophy and training methods as a coach which involved extreme dedication to the sport and a Spartan lifestyle.

At Portsea, Cerutty preached a holistic strategy involving different forms of running training, weight lifting, diet and a way of life dedicated to maximising the potential of his athletes. His overriding principle was of a 'natural' attitude to training, which flew in the face of Gerschler's allegedly rigid, scientific formulae. Cerutty disliked interval running on the track and his coaching methods took the form of runs over gruelling circuits on rough terrain and, most famously, hill running intervals on the dunes of Portsea. This form of training became a talking point for Scottish football fans years later when it was adopted by the Rangers manager, Jock Wallace, for pre-season training on the beach at Gullane in East Lothian.

Cerutty is best known for coaching Herb Elliott who set a world mile record of 3 minutes 54.5 seconds at Santry Stadium in Dublin in 1958 with four others, two of whom were also acolytes of Cerutty, breaking the four minute barrier in the same race. Elliott went on to win the Olympic 1,500 metres in Rome in 1960 in a world record of 3 minutes 35.6 seconds. He was never beaten in a mile or 1,500 metres race and had retired from athletics by the age of 24 in 1962. Cerutty was later fascinated to be told that Elliott had been motivated by the fear of defeat during his running career, rather than the overwhelming self-confidence which Cerutty thought he had instilled in him.

Cerutty also coached Albie Thomas, a multiple world record holder at imperial distances, and was involved in the careers of John Landy and Betty Cuthbert, the triple sprint champion from the Melbourne Olympics in 1956, who was also the 400 metre gold medallist in Tokyo in 1964.

LYDIARD

By the 1960s interval running was the main training preserve of middle distance runners when a former marathon and ultra runner from New Zealand called Arthur Lydiard, who had competed in the Empire Games marathon in 1950, wrote his book on distance training, 'Run to the Top', published in 1962, which almost overnight became the 'Bible' for long distance runners all over the world. Lydiard's approach was rooted in periodisation, or phases of different aspects of training, and was best known for the initial period of base work which involved running 100 miles a week. Suddenly runners everywhere were talking about mileage. If you couldn't cope with Lydiard's optimum schedule of 100 you could at least aim for 50 or 75 or 90 miles a week. Throw in some *fartlek* and you had a tried and tested formula you could rely on and experiment with, without any further need for coaching, ideal for cross country running, 5,000 metres and 10,000 metres on the track and, ultimately, the marathon.

Lydiard's methods were hugely successful in ensuring that his athletes targeted and peaked for important races. Nevertheless, it seems remarkable that his most famous *protégé*, Peter Snell, was the world's best 800 metres runner when his training was based on running 100 miles a week. This was an extreme example of what multiple World and Olympic Champion sprinter Michael Johnson refers to as 'speed endurance'. It was Snell's background in stamina work that gave him the edge in the final sprint – he wasn't speeding up, but rather he was able to sustain the same speed longer than his rivals. It is interesting to note that virtually every top class 800 metres race is run with a faster first lap. With his background of distance training, Snell was able to maintain his effort over the second lap, which was the key to his success. He was Olympic champion at 800 metres in 1960, beating the overwhelming favourite, Roger Moens, on the tape, and followed that up with an 800 metres/1,500 metres double in Tokyo four years later. He set world mile and 800 metres records on grass tracks in Wanganui and Christchurch, New Zealand in 1962, and lowered the mile time further, to 3:54.1, in Auckland in 1964.

Lydiard had many other *protégés* including Murray Halberg, Barry Magee and John Davies, all Olympic medallists, and countless adherents all over the world who read his book and followed his ideology.

The Lydiard approach to training was much more time consuming than interval running and seemed a million miles away from the Oxbridge approach. Now runners were 'taking it seriously' and were often perceived as compensating for lack of talent by their peers in other events. This class system in athletics pervaded the teams of the 1960s and could result in a polarisation between the sprinters, the throwers, the jumpers and the long distance 'plodders'. Away from sport, the idea of competition became frowned upon by many in the counter culture of the 1960s and it took a combination of extreme dedication, rigid, almost blinkered, focus and occasional social contortions, in order to live a relatively normal life on 70 miles a week, far less study for finals or hold down a 9 to 5 job.

There are a number of other well-known coaches of the post-war period including Mihály Iglói, who was mentor to the celebrated Hungarian athletes of the 1950s, Tabori, Iharos and Rózsavölgyi, and later the American Bob Schul, winner of the Olympic 5,000 metres in 1964. Bill Bowerman in Eugene, Oregon and Frank Horwill, founder of the British Milers' Club in England, were also coaching pioneers in their own way. However, for the Edinburgh students, Cerutty and Lydiard had set the ground rules for training and one athlete in particular was to be inspired by their innovative ideas to achieve a level of performance which was a revelation for Scottish running and, more importantly, a huge influence on others who followed him and attempted to emulate his achievements.

Paavo Nurmi of Finland wins the Olympic 1,500 metres in Paris in 1924 from Schärer of Switzerland and Stallard of Great Britain.
(Photographer unknown)

Rudolph Harbig illustrates his superiority over his contemporaries in an 800 metre race at the Olympic Stadium in Berlin in the 1930s.
(Photographer unknown)

I

Emil Zatopek leads Alain Mimoun and Herbert Schade past the unfortunate Chris Chataway on the final bend of the Olympic 5,000 metres in Helsinki, 1952. This was the first of three gold medals won by Zatopek at these Games.
(Photographer unknown)

Vladimir Kuts of USSR, the eventual winner, leads from Gordon Pirie of Great Britain and Dave Power of Australia in the 10,000 metres at the Olympic Games in Melbourne, 1956.
(AFP/Getty Images)

Herb Elliott of Austalia leads from Rózsavölgyi of Hungary and Jazy of France on the way to setting a new world record of 3:35.6 in the Olympic 1,500 metres final in Rome, 1960. (IOC Olympic Museum/Getty Images)

Percy Cerutty shows Herb Elliott how to run up sand dunes at Portsea, Victoria, in the 1950s.
(Photographer unknown)

Chapter Two

THE BEAST: FERGUS MURRAY AND THE SCOTTISH DISTANCE RUNNING SCENE OF THE 1960s

'I remember clearly the running days of 50 and more years ago... the camaraderie in training and the races where we would josh and jest with even with our supposedly bitter rivals. We had a good time in athletics.....it must be much more difficult for young runners starting out now. As to why we did it, that's a much more complex question to answer...'

– Fergus Murray

* * *

When Fergus Murray was growing up in Angus in the 1950s he didn't have much of a clue about competitive athletics, but he got a 'buzz' out of the solitary activity of running. His father was a civil engineer in public works, with a background as a quarry master, and the family lived in Kingennie, near Dundee, where the young Murray would take advantage of his rural environment by slipping on his gym shoes and running alone in the fields or along the country roads. He was a fee paying pupil at Dundee High School, a grant-aided school,[6] where the main sports were cricket in the summer and rugby in the winter.

But Murray was not particularly interested in team sports, particularly the 'brutal blood sport' of rugby, and found solace in endurance events and as a member of the athletics team which competed in some inter-school competitions. As an introverted and sometimes unruly pupil, he saw the mile race as an iconic event at the school sports and realised that success in it would give him kudos within the school environment. Distance running proved to be something he was genuinely good at, and this gave him the self-confidence to start competing in regional and national events.

When he was about 17 he joined Dundee Hawkhill Harriers where he met and trained with Alistair Barrie, Alan Beattie (then the Scottish Universities half mile champion), Ron Coleman and others who

---

[6] These schools provided a middle sector of education in Scotland at the time, standing midway between local authority and wholly independent schools.

introduced him to the methods of Percy Cerutty and Arthur Lydiard. Murray bought the training manuals of these legendary coaches and put in extra sessions with half mile interval runs up the local farm tracks and back. Club nights at the Harriers involved *fartleks* and 660 yard repetition running on the new, virtually car-free, Kingsway dual carriageway on the northern edge of Dundee, generously floodlit by street lamps.

Murray was primarily interested in the ideas of Cerutty at the time and he introduced his own runs on local sand dunes and along the Barrie Burn near his home. He also passed his driving test at the age of 17 and drove to train alone on the hilly cinder path in Camperdown Park in Dundee or on the track at Caird Park.

From 1960 he started recording his sessions in a neat training diary which he kept for many years, logging miles and descriptions of the runs, and records of his competitive performances for each year. The diaries show that he started doing longer runs while he was still at school including 8 miles 'steady' and eight miles *fartlek*, and even on one occasion completing a 14 mile 'easy run'. Training was becoming progressively harder and, although by his penultimate year at school and thanks to his subscription to the Athletics Weekly magazine, which introduced him to the wider athletics community, he was beginning to have ambitions beyond his home town environment, there was no single, significant event which made him want to be a great runner. Winning the 'next race' was his primary aim and the consequences – selection for Scottish Schools or, later on, Great Britain – were secondary. He just wanted to get better. Significantly, thanks again to the reports in Athletics Weekly, 'beat Bruce Tulloh, beat Bruce Tulloh' became a mantra in his training sessions.

Success did not come easily at first and Fergus recalls seeing older runners such as John Linaker of Pitreavie Amateur Athletic Club a fields-length away in the distance in his early attempts at cross-country. He finished 33rd in the Scottish National Youths Cross Country Championships in 1960 but, come the summer of that year, the extra training he was doing on his own began to pay off when he finished second in the mile at the Scottish Schools Championships at Westerlands, Glasgow in June, in a time of 4:33.5. He represented Scotland in the mile at the Schools International against Wales that year, finishing fourth in 4:36.5 on the grass track at Goldenacre (home of the playing fields of George Heriot's School in Edinburgh), despite running with a heavy cold.

The following year, after an indifferent cross country season plagued by flu, he won the Scottish Schools mile at Goldenacre in 4:27.1, and ran 4:25.2 that year in finishing fifth in the Scottish East District senior championships. However, he was disappointed to finish fourth in a tactical race behind his younger fellow Scot Hugh Barrow[7] in the Schools International, which had now been extended to include England, at Maindy Stadium in Cardiff in July 1961.

It was at school that Murray became the subject of an article in the British Medical Journal when, as a result of running in cheap plimsolls, the trauma caused by the hammering of the blood cells in his poorly protected heels led to him passing blood in his urine. Dr Ronnie Davidson, a consultant haematologist at Dundee Royal Infirmary, who was by coincidence the brother of a neighbouring farmer, undertook a research project, which also involved Murray's fellow Hawkhill runners Barrie and Coleman, into the causes of this phenomenon which, although initially alarming, proved to be inconsequential. Proper running shoes were ordered[8].

Murray's parents were not interested in running *per se* but were very supportive of what he was doing and his mother kept all his press cuttings during his running career. He was not, perhaps, particularly aware that his parents, who were funding his university education, albeit with some grant assistance, might have thought that he should be spending more time on his studies and less on an activity which was unlikely to lead to the career path that it might today. He didn't follow athletics much during the heyday of Roger Bannister and Chris Chataway but Gordon Pirie was a particular hero. Although there wasn't a great deal of press coverage that he was aware of, he recalls seeing Pirie on television going through the first mile of a three miles in 4:30 which he thought was incredible, but which proved a portent of his own achievements only a few years later.

---

[7] Hugh Barrow set a world best mile time for a 16 year old of 4:10.9 in Dublin in August 1961. Barrow's career best mile time was 4:1.0, set in 1968.

[8] I had a similar experience several years later when, after running in bare feet in the 5,000 metres at a British League race on a 'Tartan' track in Manchester, I passed blood in my urine in a pub in Penrith on the bus trip back to Edinburgh. However, after reminding myself of Fergus's experience, nothing was done about it and things soon went back to normal. Nowadays a doctor would probably be consulted.

THE EUHH PERIOD

When it came to deciding where to go to University in 1961, Edinburgh won hands down over St Andrews, but it was primarily for the running rather than for his chosen academic course of Chemistry, a subject which had captured his imagination at school and was not merely a means of gaining access to a university education. At Edinburgh, Murray was introduced to the influential Chris Elson and other freshman athletes, and to first team members including Doug Dingwall, Mike Hartley and Tony Yates, the latter a leading junior steeplechaser.

Chris came from Rotherham and brought with him an extensive knowledge of training gleaned from his clubmate Alan Simpson who was one of the leading UK milers at the time and went on to finish fourth in the Olympic 1,500 metres in Tokyo in 1964. Chris organised hill running and repetitions and was the instigator of the EUHH training camp held before the start of the academic year at Cockburnspath, down the east coast from Edinburgh in the Scottish Borders. Later on it switched to Firbush Point on Loch Tay which, from rudimentary beginnings, became the Edinburgh University Outdoor Centre. In Fergus's opinion, Chris unwittingly had the biggest impact on the success of Edinburgh University Hare and Hounds during the 1960s and beyond, taking the club, through his enthusiasm and innovative training methods, from a group of 'fun loving medical students' to one of the pre-eminent cross country teams in Britain.

Season 1961-62 was a time of steady development for Murray in his first year at university as he stepped up to an average of 30 miles a week in training. He was seventh fastest on the fourth stage of the Edinburgh to Glasgow Relay with the EUHH team finishing ninth. Then, despite finishing a disappointing 18th in the Scottish National Junior Cross Country Championships at Hamilton Racecourse, he showed his potential on the road, coming home in the lead on the first leg of the Hyde Park Relay[9] with the fifth fastest individual time of 14:17, over a

---

[9] The Hyde Park Relay was first hosted by Imperial College, London, in the late 1940s and the event remains a popular fixture of the student road running calendar to this day. It is open to university students and their alumni from the UK and beyond and, in line with the status of the hosts, the traditionally powerful Oxford, Cambridge and London Universities are represented by their colleges, rather than competing as full university teams. The race follows a route along tarmac paths in one of the most famous public open spaces in the world, passing well known sights including The Serpentine, Marble Arch and Hyde Park Corner. After the race, athletes head to Imperial College for the presentation ceremony and meal, followed by a legendary after-race party at the renowned Metric nightclub. A feature of the event is that photographs of every runner competing are offered for sale after the race.

distance of approximately three miles. Herb Elliott, running for Jesus College, Cambridge, was fourth fastest overall in 14:09.

The Edinburgh team had travelled down to London on the morning of the race in what was Murray's first flight. He admits now that his restless excitement at this experience must have been an embarrassment to the more senior members of the EUHH team, but perhaps the overall adventure contributed to his performance in the event itself which was some way better than that of his supposed superiors. The team finished a creditable seventh in a field of 88 in a time of 90:43, averaging 15:07 per leg.

In May 1962 Fergus ran a 4:21.4 mile in the Edinburgh University Sports on the undulating grass track laid out on the playing fields at Craiglockhart.[10] He was also third in the three miles at the Scottish Universities Athletics Championships, again at Craiglockhart, in 14:23.0, behind Calum Laing of Glasgow, the leading University distance runner in Scotland at that time, and Martin Craven, a stalwart of the Edinburgh team and later a leading marathon runner.

For a first year student Murray managed to achieve a commendable fifth place in the three miles at the British Universities Sports Federation Championships in May in a personal best of 14:22.0, following this up with further improvement to 14:19.7 as a guest in the Scottish Amateur Athletics Association versus Atalanta[11] match at Pitreavie on 4 July 1962. In

---

[10] The Edinburgh University playing fields at Craiglockhart were on land owned by the Edinburgh Merchant Company, who administer the nearby George Watson's College and several other fee paying schools in the city. The walled and tree-lined grounds had the benefit of an iconic Victorian timber pavilion consisting of changing rooms and spectator facilities and a clock tower which added significantly to the atmosphere for athletics meetings and rugby matches. When part of the land was released for housing, the Edinburgh University Athletic Club (now the Edinburgh University Sports Union) relocated its facilities in 1969 to its own grounds at Peffermill where a new cinder track was laid. However, the new development came in for some criticism as, not only did it lack the atmosphere of Craiglockhart, but it was on a much more exposed site. More importantly, perhaps, all-weather tracks in Tartan [such as the one at the National Sports Centre at Crystal Palace in London, which became the home of British Athletics after the demise of the White City] and similar materials were beginning to be developed at this time and it was felt that, with their anachronistic approach, an opportunity was being missed by EUAC, despite the potential additional costs involved.

[11] The Atalanta Athletic Club, founded in 1925, was a composite team represented by the four ancient Scottish universities of St Andrews, Glasgow, Aberdeen, and Edinburgh. It was the Scottish equivalent of the Achilles Club which was founded in 1920 for past and present members of Oxford and Cambridge University Athletic Clubs. Atalanta is no longer extant and the last official record of its involvement in competition is the match against the Scottish Amateur Athletic Association at Grangemouth in June 1969.

the latter race, which John Linaker won in 13:48.0, Murray went through two miles in another personal best of 9:19.4 but his training diary reveals that he 'blew up' having been too ambitious with his early pace.

More significantly, however, Fergus Murray confirmed the extent of his competitive ambition by joining Ilford Athletic Club at the end of the summer term. He ran for them regularly over the vacation, further reducing his three mile time to 14:14.0 at the club's home track at Cricklefield Stadium in an inter-club event later in July. He also lowered his best mile time to 4:19.4 running for Ilford at a meeting in Ipswich on 21 July, which was held on a grass track. The move south was the result of a chance meeting at Kinlochleven Highland Games with one of the Essex club's leading distance runners, Dennis Plater, a 2:20 marathon man, who was holidaying in Scotland that summer. With the Plater family providing the hospitality, and Fergus the performances on the track and the roads, the experiment was repeated in 1963, 1964 and for a time in 1965, and he also represented Ilford in a number of subsequent events.

Racing opportunities, more competition and better weather conditions ensured that this was an enterprising move for an aspiring young Scottish distance runner with time on his hands during the summer holidays. It also allowed him contact with important role models in the Essex area including Mel Batty, who was a member of Thurrock Harriers, the American Leonard 'Buddy' Edelen, the first sub-2 hour 15 minute marathon runner, who competed for Chelmsford Athletic Club, and Alan Perkins, who won the English National Cross Country title, running for Ilford, in 1958. Through time, as he improved, Fergus found the environment in the south of England, and the races and trips abroad, much more stimulating than competition in Scotland.

Back in Scotland in August 1962, the Ilford experience clearly appeared to be paying off, with fourth place in the two miles at Edinburgh Highland Games at Murrayfield Stadium, the home of Scottish Rugby, in a significant personal best of 9:05.4. The race was won in 8:53.4 by Bruce Tulloh, who had just become the European 5,000 metres champion. In the autumn, barely 20 years old, Fergus ran the second fastest individual leg (to Andy Brown of Motherwell YMCA Harriers) at the first major fixture of the winter season, the Macandrew Road Relay in Glasgow, and set an individual course record of 13:10 in the Kingsway Relays in his home town of Dundee, by now back running for EUHH. Then, in November 1962, he exposed himself to a new challenge by finishing fifth in the Brampton to Carlisle 10 mile road race in 50:13 over a distance which, on the track, was shortly to give him the grounding to succeed at 10,000 metres. Andy

Brown was the winner in 48:37 and Murray logged his own performance as 'a reasonable run'.

It should be noted that, until the start of the 'jogging boom' in the late 1970s, road races generally were run over approximate and mostly non-standard distances. Although, for example, the Nigel Barge was described as 'four and a half miles', the Windermere to Kendal (which was originally run on the main A591 road through the South Lakes) 'eight miles', the Brampton to Carlisle 'ten miles', and the Edinburgh to North Berwick 'twenty two miles' (later extended to the full marathon distance and then subsequently reduced to the exact standard distance of 20 miles, on a new course from Portobello Promenade), none of these distances was exact.

The classic Morpeth to Newcastle Road Race, run on the first of January each year, was measured at 13.6 miles, eschewing the opportunity to make it an exact half marathon distance until it was standardised in 2002. This was probably the result of commercial pressure as, by the 2000s, runners, willing to pay relatively hefty entry fees, with the added bonus of a free T shirt and a sponsor's bottle of mineral water, were more interested in testing themselves as individuals against the clock over accurate distances. This allowed comparison with other courses and the opportunity to monitor progress, rather than racing over approximate distances on the road or the country where competition between runners and teams had traditionally been the purpose of the exercise. These approximations did not, however, apply to marathons which have, since the Olympic Games in 1924, always been run over the exact distance of 26 miles 385 yards.

Murray thrived at shorter distances over the 1962-63 season, running the fastest leg in the East District Relays, finishing first equal, with Jim McLatchie of Ayr Seaforth, in the annual Scottish Cross Country Union versus Scottish Universities match in December 1962, and winning the Nigel Barge Road Race in January 1963 from McLatchie and 19-year-old Lachie Stewart. However, he also suffered from colds and flu over the winter period, a consequence he feels of his intensive training regime, which prevented him from competing that winter in the Edinburgh to Glasgow Relay, the East District and British Universities Championships, and the Hyde Park Relay.

Things returned to normal in February 1963 when Murray won the Scottish National Junior Cross Country title by the huge margin of 31 seconds from Mike Ryan of St Modans (later to win the bronze medal in

23

the 1968 Olympic marathon in Mexico City, competing for New Zealand), with the EUHH team winning the first of three successive team titles. Unfortunately, a further attack of flu prevented him from competing in the International Cross Country Championships in San Sebastian, although he did manage to take up an invitation to the prestigious Martini International Cross Country race in Brussels at the end of the winter season.

The early summer of 1963 brought numerous successes including his first sub-14 minute three miles, finishing second in 13:52.6 behind Ron Hill at the British Universities Championships at Motspur Park, Surrey in May (with Martin Craven third in 13:56.6), and best championship performances for the three miles at the Edinburgh University Sports, with 14:26.8 (beating Adrian Jackson's record of 14:29), and the East District Championships, with 14:07.6. He followed these successes up with a significant victory in the Scottish Championships at Westerlands in late June in 14:01.6, well ahead of Andy Brown who had won the six miles, after a distance running 'war of attrition' with John Linaker, the previous evening. Murray then reduced his personal best to 13:49.0 running for Atalanta against the SAAA in windy conditions at Pitreavie in early July 1963, again ahead of the ubiquitous and peerlessly consistent Brown.

Down at Ilford in the summer of 1963, Murray lowered his mile best to 4:12.2 in the Beverley Baxter Meeting at Southgate on 17 July. Then, three days later, running as a guest in the annual match between the British Universities, the Amateur Athletic Association and the Combined Services at Portsmouth, he made a quantum leap to 13:32.6 for three miles, challenging the barefoot Ron Hill (who had equalled the UK and Commonwealth records for 6 miles in the fourth fastest time ever at the AAA Championships earlier in the month) into the final straight in a high quality British field. This was a major achievement for a Scottish runner and was basically his breakthrough into UK level, ranking him ninth fastest for the year. It gave him the step up in confidence to go on to win three successive Scottish Senior Cross Country titles, and to compete on a par with the best distance runners in Britain for the next four or five years. At the age of 21 he was selected to run the 10,000 metres for Britain in the 1964 Olympic Games in Tokyo.

It is important to recognise that ambitious Scottish runners like Fergus Murray only considered themselves a success if they could be competitive at UK level. Selection for the Olympic Games was the distance runner's overriding aim and it was a British, not a Scottish, team which competed there. Moreover, better to be a big fish in a big pond, than a big fish in a wee one.

He rounded off the summer of 1963 at Ilford with another personal best, this time in a two mile race at Slough on 3 August with 8:53.6, ahead of the 1962 English Cross Country Champion Gerry North, and second place to Mel Batty, another English distance running legend, in the Hadleigh 6 mile road race. On his return to Scotland, tired after his efforts in the south, Fergus finished down the field in the two mile race at Edinburgh Highland Games on the five laps to a mile grass track at Murrayfield, which was won by Gaston Roelants of Belgium, then the European Steeplechase Champion.

Training was becoming very serious. There was none of the student drinking culture which became prevalent in the University team in the late 1960s. Although his mileage for most of that summer was relatively modest by his later standards, by the end of 1963 Murray was often running over 70 miles a week and became known as 'The Beast' for the extent and intensity of his training[12]. Driven by the desire to improve and succeed at UK level, he had the good fortune to avoid injuries, with one significant exception, as well as the mental and physical strength to sustain this level of training, much of which was on roads, for almost 10 years.

He was almost wholly self coached, pointing out in *'Who's Who in British Athletics'* in the Athletics Weekly of 6 March 1965 that his main inspiration came from 'my club mates among whom we have critical appreciations of training'. Frank Dick and John Anderson were the foremost Scottish athletics coaches around this time, and for many years thereafter, but although he consulted them from time to time they perhaps did not command sufficient respect among distance runners primarily because, unlike Cerutty and Lydiard, they had never been distance runners themselves[13].

Over the winter of 1963-64, Fergus built on his successful summer, averaging 58 miles per week in training for the full year. He ran the fastest leg in the East District Relays and fastest in the tough second stage of

---

[12] The relatively hirsute Chris Elson, himself a talented although sadly unfulfilled athlete, meanwhile had to make do with 'The Bear'.

[13] Anderson and Dick later became well known to a wider public in other spheres, Anderson as the referee in the TV series 'Gladiators' with his mantra 'Contenders ready!' and Dick as fitness coach to multiple Grand Slam-winning tennis player Boris Becker, and subsequently as a much sought-after motivational speaker.

the Edinburgh to Glasgow Relay, with the EUHH team winning the 'Most Meritorious Award', for the most improved team, in fifth place. A course record of 25:20 for the EUHH cross country course from the Edinburgh science campus at King's Buildings followed, before he finished in second place in the 'Brampton' in 47:12 to Jim Alder's winning time of 47:06. This was an improvement of over three minutes on his previous attempt at this event only a year earlier.

On New Year's Day 1964, running for Dundee Hawkhill, he finished third in the Morpeth to Newcastle road race behind John Anderson of Saltwell Harriers and Jim Alder, the local Morpeth Harrier, in 1:06:54. This was his first attempt at this classic race which he was to run six times in total, winning twice, and finishing second twice and third twice. He followed this up a few days later with second in the Nigel Barge (having gone off course when in the lead), first in the East Districts Championships from his old teammate Ron Coleman and first in the Scottish Universities Cross Country Championships at St Andrews, by 51 seconds, from Calum Laing of Glasgow, despite again going off course on several occasions during the race due to poor marking.

In February 1964 Fergus Murray and Mike Turner of Cambridge University (who a few weeks later was to finish second to Mel Batty in the English Cross Country Championships) ran in together in first place in the British Universities Cross Country Championships in Nottingham, with EUHH finishing 11th in the team race. The result was another invitation to the 'Martini' where Murray finished third behind the host's favourite, Gaston Roelants, and his soon-to-be 5,000 metres rival Derek Graham of Northern Ireland. The Hyde Park Relay, where Edinburgh finished ninth, was another battle with Turner, with the Liverpudlian running the fastest leg of 13:36 to Murray's 13:39, both well inside the then individual course record of 13:57 held by English cross country international Tim Briault.

Out of loyalty to his old club (and given the EUHH senior team's slim chances of making any impact) Murray ran for Dundee Hawkhill in the Scottish National Senior Cross Country Championships on the heavy grass surface at Hamilton Racecourse on 29 February 1964, winning the first of his three successive titles effortlessly, and by the considerable margin of 39 seconds, from Jim Alder. According to his training diary entry the race 'went like a song'. However, following victory in the Windermere to Kendal on 14 March (by nearly a minute over the eight mile course) he ran below par in the International Cross Country Championships at the Leopardstown Racecourse in Dublin, finishing 40th (fourth Scot), with Scotland a disappointing seventh in the team race.

Fergus Murray never ran to his full potential in the International, despite his stellar performances at the 'Scottish' and the British Universities, perhaps because the courses, which often had hurdles and other man-made obstacles, did not suit him. However, a more compelling reason was that the International was the last event in a long winter season in which he raced and trained relentlessly. In the 1964 International race he complained of tiredness in his legs which resulted in him stopping to take off his shoes and running in bare feet, a decision which he felt probably cost him as many as 20 places by the finish.

After the disappointment of the International, Murray recovered his resolve to put in an excellent and, as it transpired, hugely significant performance in the AAA Ten Miles at Hurlingham in April in the wake of Mel Batty's world record of 47:26.8, running inside the Olympic qualifying time for 10,000 metres and setting new Scottish records for every distance from four miles to 10 miles *en route*. Following the inspirational Batty's lead he went through the first five miles in an ambitious 23:40, paving the way for the important splits of 28:29.4 at six miles and 29:33.8 at 10,000 metres, before finishing in 48:41. There is little doubt that he would have run considerably faster for the overall distance with more even splits, but he might not have achieved the intermediate qualifying time had he adopted such a strategy. In any case he was more engaged with the race against Batty and even-paced running was just not in his nature in such a competitive situation.

He still had time for a sprinkling of university and other local races, which he continued to train through, including performances as diverse as the Clydebank to Helensburgh 16 mile road race on 25 April, which he won by nearly two minutes, and an impressive personal best (especially considering the track) of 4:08.2 for the mile in the match against Edinburgh Southern Harriers and Durham University at Craiglockhart on 16 May. In the mile race he finished ahead of Kenny Ballantyne of 'Southern' who went on to win the Scottish title in this event the following month.

Although Fergus Murray made the British Olympic team in 1964 as a 10,000 metres runner, much to the chagrin at the time of established English runners like Mike Freary and Martyn Hyman, it was at 3 miles/5,000 metres[14] that his athletics career really took off. The other contenders for the Olympic team in the shorter event were Mike Wiggs

---

[14] The accepted convention is to add 28 seconds to a three mile time to establish the comparative performance at international level for 5,000 metres. Similarly, 60 seconds is added to the six mile time to establish the equivalent 10,000 metres time.

(who would replace Gordon Pirie as the British record holder for the distance the following year), 1962 European Champion Bruce Tulloh, the Northern Irishman Derek Graham and John 'Kipper' Herring of Blackheath Harriers, and an intense battle for selection was played out by these five adversaries throughout the summer of 1964.

Fergus, spurred on by his performance at Hurlingham, set the ball rolling with a personal best for 5,000 metres of 13:58.4 at the Leyton Floodlit Meeting on 6 May, ahead of John Cooke of Portsmouth and Mel Batty. He followed this up with a 13:35.2 three mile victory over Tim Johnston at the British Universities Championships on 23 May, before finishing second in the mile the following afternoon. Tulloh, meanwhile, won the English Inter-Counties three miles (which was regarded, in the British 'scene', as second only to the AAA Championships in prestige at that time) on 16 May in 13:23.6, ahead of Herring in 13:28.4.

However, Wiggs virtually guaranteed his Olympic selection by winning the Southern AAA three miles on 20 June in 13:16.6, tenth fastest of all time, and Tulloh faltered as a result of an attack of measles, leaving Murray, Herring and Graham as the main contenders for the remaining two places. At the AAA Championships at the White City Stadium in July, Murray entered for both the three miles and the six miles, with the six being run, in accordance with tradition, on the Friday evening. This race was a classic of that period with Mike Bullivant winning in a British record time of 27:26.6 ahead of Ron Hill (27:27.0), Martin Hyman (27:36.0) and Mike Freary (27:37.6). Murray dropped out at the three mile mark in an exceedingly fast 13:45, aware that he would be sacrificing his chances in the three mile race the next day if he continued in a race in which, even at that pace, he was struggling to make a significant impact. It was a fortuitous decision as, after leading with two laps to go, he finished fifth in the 'three' in a personal best of 13:29.2, only one second adrift of Tulloh and ahead of Graham and Herring. Polish athletes filled the first two places with Tom O'Riordan of Ireland in fourth. Meanwhile Wiggs, with his selection in the 5,000 metres more or less 'in the bag', ran the mile, in which he was also a contender for the Olympic team, and finished a close second to Alan Simpson in 4:01.6 after leading into the finishing straight.

While not in the same class as Wiggs at the mile, Murray lowered his best time for the distance to 4:06.0 behind Malcolm Browne (4:05.1) at the Beverley Baxter Trophy Meeting at Broomfield Park, Enfield four days later, finding the performance 'effortless' and giving him more confidence in his basic speed, and aspirations to a time closer to four minutes that season[15].

As a result of his run in the AAA Championships, Fergus was selected as a travelling reserve for a trip to Helsinki for the Britain against Finland match on 22 July. Wiggs and Tulloh were scheduled to run in the 5,000 metres but Wiggs pulled out with shoulder and neck pains, the result of a fall in training, and Murray was called in to compete at the last minute. Despite training hard over seven miles the day before (and having been out for a five mile run with Ron Hill and Mel Batty on the day of the race itself) he not only won in a personal best, but also realised his ambition from several years earlier by finishing ahead of Tulloh for the first time, setting a new track record of 13:49.0 for the stadium where, at this distance 12 years earlier, the legendary Zatopek had won the second of his three Olympic gold medals. Only Gordon Pirie, Stan Eldon and Mike Wiggs among British runners had run faster and Tulloh's time of 13:49.4 was also a personal best although it was inferior to his three mile time of 13:12.0 set in Southampton in 1961. It is possible that Murray's performance benefitted from his last minute inclusion in the race, which would have taken the pressure off him due to the reduced expectation, but nevertheless this was another major breakthrough in his running career.

Graham meanwhile had run two top class races in Ireland that summer, 13:18.4 for three miles in narrowly winning the All Ireland Championships at Santry Stadium in Dublin on 20 June, from the Republic's O'Riordan, then 13:18.8 on 14 July, again at Santry and again from O'Riordan. These were performances clearly deserving of selection, but they would have been more persuasive had they been run in the UK where Graham's times, while extremely competitive, were less convincing[16].

The final opportunities to impress the selectors were the Bank Holiday meetings at Crystal Palace on Saturday 1 August and the White City on the following Monday. On the Saturday, Herring won the 5,000 metres in 13:58.6 from Graham (14:01.2) and Murray (14:05.8), with Tulloh, weakened by illness, dropping out. On the Monday at the White City

---

[15] It was not to be. This was Murray's career-best time for the mile.

[16] This view is supported by the editorial comment in Athletics Weekly, following the announcement of the British team for Tokyo, which perhaps betrayed a Southern bias by stating that it was 'difficult to understand the reasoning behind the selections of Graham and Murray in the 5k and 10k respectively'.

(it was intense in those days) it was Graham's turn to lead the Great Britain and Northern Ireland runners home as he finished second to Lech Boguszewicz of Poland in 13:59.4 with Herring third, despite a fall, Murray fourth and Wiggs, with his selection secure, well down in sixth in 14:24.

Tulloh then came up with a late flourish to impress the selectors with 13:19.0 for three miles, running barefoot in his club championships on the grass track in Southampton on 12 August. It was far from too little but, alas for Tulloh, too late for selection.

In mid-August, Murray, on holiday back home in Angus following victory in 8:57.2 for the two miles at Edinburgh Highland Games, was perplexed and ecstatic in equal measure to receive a midnight call from Rab Forman, the Scottish representative on the British Amateur Athletic Board, confirming that he had been selected for the Olympic 10,000 metres, along with Bullivant and Hill, while Wiggs, Graham and Herring were given the nod in the five. But what was the logic of the selections? Despite his performance over 10 miles at Hurlingham in April, Fergus Murray had only completed one 6 mile/10,000 metres event prior to his Olympic selection (the Scottish Championships 6 miles, which he won easily in 29:05.2, some way outside the Olympic qualifying standard, in late June).

His place in the 10,000 metres was clearly a consolation for not being picked for the 5,000 metres and appears to have been based on his promise at the longer event rather than a proven track record. The editorial and correspondence in 'Athletics Weekly' at the time confirmed the controversial nature of the selections in both events, commenting that: 'In the 10,000m, while appreciating what a fine prospect Fergus Murray undoubtedly is, and his determined and courageous running to date, it cannot be suggested that he has earned a Tokyo place'. The magazine, which had strong sympathies with Tulloh, even proposed that the canny and consistent 'Kipper' Herring should have been the sole automatic pick in the 5,000 metres, with the others left to race again for the remaining places in the shorter event - all this despite the large number of races already undertaken which had, from time to time, taken their toll on the likes of Wiggs and Tulloh.

Despite the controversy, prior to flying out to Tokyo, Fergus was greatly relieved to set a Scottish record of 29:10.4 in finishing second to Ron Hill in the 10,000 metres for Britain against France on the Friday evening of a two-day international at a 'magical', floodlit White City in

September (with another Scottish National record of 28:11.8 for six miles *en route*). On this occasion he burnt off the opposition with a 64 second penultimate lap, going a long way towards vindicating his selection in an event in which he was later to have considerable success.

Murray's inclusion in the Olympic team possibly also owed a great deal to Rab Forman who was often instrumental in drawing the selectors' attention to the candidacy of Scottish runners, and was an extremely persuasive advocate for Scottish athletics.

Not surprisingly, given the effort made just to qualify for the Games, Tokyo was a disappointment in running terms for Fergus Murray and the other British distance men. Murray, suffering from a heavy cold, finished 22nd in the 10,000 metres, behind Hill and Bullivant who were 18th and 21st respectively. In the 5,000 metres, of the British runners only Wiggs qualified for the final but he tripped and fell early in the race, which was run in a heavy downpour, and trailed home in 11th place. However, for an inexperienced athlete like Fergus Murray, who a little over two years earlier had finished well down the field in the Scottish Junior Cross Country Championships, it was an eye opener to see what could be achieved by increased training and careful planning. More importantly, perhaps, it was inspirational to be in the company of the great runners of the time, Ron Clarke and Kip Keino, Michel Jazy and Mohammed Gammoudi, Abebe Bikila and Peter Snell, and the Americans Schul, who outpsyched Jazy and company to win the 5,000 metres,[17] and Mills, who surprised everyone, including himself, with his victory in the 10.

With his status in British distance running assured, and with the confidence and sense of well-being engendered by his successful track season, Fergus's training went extremely well over the winter of 1964-65. On 7 November he completed 105 miles of training for the week with first place in an East District League race in Hawick, just two seconds ahead of Craig Douglas of the local Teviotdale Harriers[18]. Tellingly, his

---

[17] Looking back, Schul should perhaps have been taken more seriously. He was top of the 5,000 metres rankings, at 13:38.0, before the Games [Mel Watman had earmarked him for victory in his predictions in Athletics Weekly] and he had a blistering finish which he used to devastating effect with a 38.5 second final 300 metres in the Tokyo final. The indifferent early pace set by Ron Clarke, possibly drained by his unexpected defeat in the 10,000 metres, clearly played into Schul's hands.

[18] Craig Douglas later joined Edinburgh Southern Harriers in order to get more competition on the track. He was particularly successful in British League races at 800 metres and 1,500 metres in the 1970s.

diary records that it was a 'fast trail but had many fences which I climbed and Craig Douglas vaulted, resulting in a much harder race than I would have wanted'. The East District League consisted of three races spread throughout each cross country season. It was an ideal platform for runners to test their fitness and it provided competitive training opportunities over courses of differing lengths and surfaces, from the fences and hills of Hawick to the mud and plough of Newcraighall in Edinburgh, or the varied terrain at Grangemouth or Musselburgh.

Two weeks after the Hawick race the EUHH team made a well-deserved breakthrough to finish second to Motherwell YMCA Harriers in the Edinburgh to Glasgow Relay with Fergus Murray fastest on the second leg in 29:18 ahead of Hugh Barrow of Victoria Park AAC (29:38) and Mel Edwards of Aberdeen AC (29:43), again despite a heavy cold. At that time the second leg, although shorter than the sixth, was considered the classy leg, where the main individual runners went head to head.

1964 was signed off on 28 November with first equal, with Ian McCafferty, for Scotland in the annual cross country fixture against the Army. In the typical week's training leading up to this race, (from 22 to 28 November 1964) he ran over 100 miles, consisting of:

> **Sunday** – a.m. 12.5 miles steady with Roger Young, Jim Wight and Alex Wight; p.m. 9.5 miles steady on road; **Monday** – a.m. 4 miles steady (to King's Buildings); p.m. 11 miles *fartlek* with Roger Young; evening 7 miles *fartlek*; **Tuesday** – a.m. 4 miles steady (to KB); p.m. 9 miles steady with Roger Young and Chris Elson; **Wednesday** – a.m. 4 miles steady (to KB); p.m. 12 miles *fartlek* with EUHH team; **Thursday** - a.m. 4 miles steady (to KB); p.m. 10 miles *fartlek* with Chris Elson; **Friday** – 8 miles steady; **Saturday** – Scotland versus The Army – 6 miles.

(In his training diary for this week he also notes that one of his knees is causing some discomfort and he receives heat treatment at the University Health Centre which was very supportive of EUHH runners at the time.)

The Morpeth to Newcastle on 1 January 1965 was 'not too serious a race' on this occasion as he finished well behind Jim Alder, winner in 1:05:42, a course record by 21 seconds, with Mike Gowan of Herne Hill Harriers second in 1:06:02 and Murray a comfortable third in 1:07:26, after easing off when he realised that it was not his day. It was an occasion when Alder, anxious to avoid being outsprinted by the 21 year old Gowan, who was to run 4:01 for the mile later that year, pushed the pace from the gun and Murray 'just let him go' after four miles. The Nigel Barge a few days later was an altogether closer affair as Murray finished second in 22:33 to McCafferty's record breaking victory in 22:29. He then won the East District Championships from teammate Roger Young on 16 January and the Scottish Universities from Bill Ewing of Aberdeen University and Chris Elson a week later.

It was typical of Fergus Murray to fit a prolific number of races, many of them minor club events, within such a gruelling training schedule. This would have required considerable mental strength and he admits he often had to psych himself up, even for training, particularly if he was doing the long Sunday runs in the Pentlands on his own.

The training was paying off, however, and the British Universities Championships on 6 February in Nottingham produced yet another epic battle with Mike Turner, the lead changing hands several times before the Cambridge man prevailed, with Murray second in the same time of 27:42. A measure of the superiority of these two great runners can be seen in the distance they had over the field with John Jackson of Liverpool University, one of England's top steeplechasers and himself a leading British distance runner, one minute behind in third. EUHH were fifth in the team race.

Two weeks later Fergus won the second of his three successive Scottish Senior Cross Country titles at Hamilton Racecourse, leading the field from the gun and eventually finishing 24 seconds ahead of Jim Alder, representing Edinburgh Athletic Club, despite the Morpeth man breaking clear of the chasing pack in an attempt to catch him. Lachie Stewart finished third. Unfortunately, Fergus was again unable to reproduce such outstanding form at the International in Ostend where the heavy going put paid to his chances after he was well up with the leaders, eventually finishing second of the Scottish contingent in 39th place.

Undeterred, he emerged from his intense winter's training in May 1965, entering for the Shettleston Marathon in Glasgow on a whim to test his fitness. After running with the vastly experienced marathon man Alastair Wood of Aberdeen[19] up to the 18 mile mark, Fergus broke clear and went on to win the race in the then spectacular time of 2:18:30,

---

[19] Among his many great achievements, Alastair Wood finished fourth for Britain in the European Marathon Championships in Belgrade in 1962. He set a European best time for the marathon in the Inverness to Forres race in 1966. Wood was largely responsible for the popularity of the event in the Aberdeen area which produced many top class runners including Mel Edwards, Steve Taylor, Colin Youngson, Graham Laing, Sandy Keith, Rab Heron and Fraser Clyne.

which was to rank him fifth in Britain for the year, and ninth on the British All-Time list at that time. Wood was not far behind in 2:19:03.

University competition continued to provide Fergus with opportunities to experiment with racing strategies and he even managed to engage in '(playing) around, stopping, sprinting, running' and allegedly performing a forward roll in the outside lane, as he teamed up with Roger Young to win the three miles in 14:55 for Edinburgh University against Glasgow in the annual Appleton Trophy meeting at Craiglockhart on 22 May, after having won the mile in 4:17.2 earlier in the afternoon. Fortunately, the affable and lamented Jim Bogan, running for Glasgow, saw the fun in this despite the fact that, as an example of sportsmanship, it didn't go down well with some of the EUAC officials.

A week later later, Murray, brave, determined and ambitious, only his bright red face betraying the effort, more than emulated his hero Pirie by going through the first mile of the East District three miles at Meadowbank Stadium[20] in 4:24 and, in unseasonably warm conditions and on a geriatric cinder track, he went on to set a Scottish Native record of 13:25.4, the equivalent of 13:53 for 5,000 metres. In the week leading up to this there was little respite in training. He ran a total of 81 miles, including 25 miles on the Pentland Hills on the Sunday, just over a week after his marathon debut, an interval training session on the Thursday and three miles on the Braid Hills on the morning of the race, which was a regular feature of his training regime. The day after this record breaking performance, on Sunday 30 May 1965, he was back over the Pentlands for another 25 miles.

***

But Fergus Murray didn't always have things his own way in Scotland at this time. Lachie Stewart and Jim Alder were beginning to carve out their

---

[20] Meadowbank was known as 'New Meadowbank' at the time as it had been built next to the original speedway track and football stadium of 'Old Meadowbank' in the 1930s. It was completely redeveloped for the Commonwealth Games in 1970, and was the venue for many international athletics events throughout the 1970s and 80s. Michael Johnston, Olympic and World Champion and world record holder over 200 metres and 400 metres, ran under 20 seconds for the 200 metres for the first time in his career on this track with a time of 19.85 seconds in cool, damp and blustery conditions on 6 July 1990. Since then, Meadowbank Stadium, which is currently the home ground of Edinburgh City Football Club, has gone into long term decline, although the track is still used for minor events and for athletics training. Further redevelopment has been mooted for some time but currently Scotland does not have a dedicated stadium capable of hosting international athletics.

own stellar careers and Andy Brown, John Linaker and Alastair Wood were among the established, older runners who were still a force to be reckoned with in the early to mid-1960s. Moreover, two younger runners from EUHH's main adversaries at the time, Motherwell YMCA Harriers, emerged in the form of Alex Brown, younger brother of Andy, and Ian McCafferty.

Alex Brown never really fulfilled his potential after his successful early years, when he was top of the British junior rankings at three miles, despite frequently having to race in indifferent weather on inferior, often home-made, tracks and in low quality races which very often provided the only competition in Scotland after the National Championships in June each year. Ian McCafferty, on the other hand, went on to become one of the finest, and perhaps most talented, home-produced Scottish distance runners of all time. He first broke through as a 19 year old in 1964, winning the International Junior Cross Country title in Dublin and, by the following year, had run the two miles in 8:42.2 and the three in 13:30.0.

He became a serious rival to Fergus Murray in 1966, the year of the Commonwealth Games in Kingston, Jamaica. Part of the selection process for these Games involved a midweek three mile race at Pitreavie on 8 June in the annual East versus West District meeting where the main protagonists at the distance assembled to impress the selectors. It was seen as a match-up between the now-established Murray, still only 23 years of age, and the emerging McCafferty, and Murray outpysched his younger rival by throwing in a 62.9 second lap three from home and running the last mile in 4:19, to win in 13:26.8, with McCafferty some distance adrift in 13:37.0.

Fergus, aware of his lack of basic speed at international level, often employed the tactic of pushing the pace with several laps to go, but it was primarily of psychological benefit against runners with faster finishes, and did not necessarily make sense in terms of maximising his own effort. However, the Pitreavie race was fitting revenge after the farce of the Centenary Mile at the Edinburgh University Sports in May that year when McCafferty had won easily in 4:13.4, with Murray disappointing the expectant Craiglockhart crowd by steering clear of direct confrontation with the Motherwell runner, and finishing a distant second in 4:22.4 after effortlessly sprinting away from his young team mates, Dave Logue and me, over the final 200 metres.

But the taciturn Ian McCafferty was an enigma. As a relative unknown,

35

running easily, he led the field in the International Senior Cross Country Championships in Rabat, Morocco, in 1966 until the 5,000 metre mark, only to stop all of a sudden, allegedly to take a stone out of his shoe. Despite this, he eventually finished well up the field with Lachie Stewart, Jim Alder and the English protagonists of the day, in 14th place. The late James Coote of the Daily Telegraph, writing in Athletics Weekly, described his performance as 'a really valiant effort'.

However, McCafferty subsequently developed, however unfairly, a reputation for lacking the self-belief to match his peerless physical ability, dropping out of races when sharing the lead, reprising the 'stone in the shoe' scenario, and often finishing so far down the field that it was thought there was something physically wrong with him. The following year, at the International in Barry in South Wales, he was running in second place behind the eventual winner, Gaston Roelants of Belgium, when he fell at the water jump and dropped out at the halfway mark, a situation repeated in the 1970 championship race. Although he finished an excellent third in the International at Clydebank in 1969, behind Roelants and Dick Taylor of England, his performances in the 1965 and 1972 races were also extremely disappointing, not only for him, but also for the Scottish running community. In 1972, Scotland had been considered among the favourites to win the team race and, if Ian McCafferty had performed to script, they would at least have been assured of a bronze medal although, in fairness, other members of the team also failed to live up to expectations on that occasion.

These instances of Ian McCafferty's apparent self-doubt were of course interspersed with performances of sheer brilliance including his breakthrough as a 21 year old, running 13:12.2 for fifth place in the Commonwealth three miles in Kingston in 1966, after mixing it with Ron Clarke and Kip Keino of Kenya up to the halfway point in the race. He went on to consolidate his new-found status with a UK three mile record of 13:06.4 behind Clarke's 12:59.0 in Dublin in July 1967, only two days after setting a Scottish record over the same distance at the AAA Championships. McCafferty also held the UK two mile record with 8:33.2, set in 1967, and was the first home Scot to run a four minute mile[21] with his time of 3:56.8 set at Reading on 11 June 1969, ahead of Anglo Scots Ian and Peter Stewart.

Two of Ian McCafferty's performances in particular stand out, including

---

[21] Anglo-Scot Mike Berisford, who was born in Bucklow in Cheshire, and competed for Sale Harriers, ran a 3:59.2 mile at the White City in August 1962.

his epic 5,000 metres race at the Commonwealth Games in Edinburgh in July 1970 when, after seeing off the legendary Keino, he closed on Ian Stewart in the straight only to finish half a stride behind his Anglo-Scottish team mate. However, arguably his finest achievement was his Scottish 5,000 metres record of 13:19.8 in July 1972, chasing home Dave Bedford at the AAA Championships at Crystal Palace, London, which were doubling as the Olympic trials, in the second fastest ever 5,000 metres at that time.

The AAA race was held on the Friday evening and 'The Palace' was throbbing that night with an expectant crowd of fans and fellow athletes, their own events completed, assembled to witness local London lad and runners' runner Bedford, still smarting from his defeat in the European 10,000 metres the year before, have a go at Ron Clarke's world record with his flamboyant front running. Characteristically, Bedford hauled the field through a 4:11 first mile and built up a lead of over 40 metres at the 3,000 metre point, reached in 7:53.6, over three seconds faster than Clarke's equivalent time in his record breaking run. Bedford was still comfortably ahead at the bell but the mercurial Scot with the devastating finish ate away at his lead and, with 200 metres to go, looked as if he might pull off an unexpected victory, only to realise that his reluctance to commit himself in the early part of the race had left him with too much to do in the home straight. Bedford, timed at 13:17.2, failed in his record bid by just 0.6 of a second. Meanwhile, Stewart, the proud Brummie-Scot, Commonwealth and former European Champion at the distance, still making his way back from long term injury, was another 40 metres back in third, despite running his second fastest ever time for the distance.

Ian McCafferty's biggest disappointment was at the Olympic Games in Munich in 1972 where, after an effortless performance in winning his 5,000 metres heat, including a last lap of 54.7 seconds, which had him labelled as one of the favourites for the Olympic title, he failed to make any impact in the final, finishing well down the field in 13:43.2. In fact, Bedford, demoralised by Lasse Viren's superiority in the 10,000 metres, also imploded in the final leaving Stewart as the most successful of the three Britons in third place despite misgivings about the colour of his medal[22]. Before the final, by then homesick and apprehensive about the pressure of expectation in the British camp, McCafferty had seemed more concerned with catching the flight home straight afterwards than

---

[22] Ian Stewart was so disappointed by his third place that he allegedly coined the phrase "first is first and second is nowhere" and was tempted to "throw [his bronze] medal over the grandstand".

engaging in the race. To add to the pressure he had also found out in a phone call home that his wife Betty was pregnant with their first child. The morning after the final, the Scottish Daily Express, having sent round a reporter to watch the race with Betty back home in Lanarkshire, ran the front page headline "Mrs McCafferty's fury – 'That's him finished with running...I wouldn't go through all that again'", going on to report "'No wonder he's hanging his head in shame', Betty said, addressing the TV screen. 'Just wait till he comes home – I'll be telling him a thing or two'". This blatant exploitation by the newspaper would not have gone down well in the McCafferty household.

Ian McCafferty was a light footed, effortlessly floating runner like the great Kenyan/Danish 800 metre runner Wilson Kipketer, or the multiple world record holder and Olympic Champion Sebastian Coe, and was much more accomplished over shorter distances than Fergus Murray, with a best mile time almost 10 seconds faster. This was a marked contrast in style from the strong man Murray. After the huge anti-climax of Munich, where he had been a genuine contender, Ian turned to pedestrianism in the hope of gaining some financial return from his talent. Professional athletics was beginning to be promoted seriously by the International Track Association around that time, and he signed a three year contract with them in September 1973. However, he ended up running in a minor handicap event on a dog track in Tranent, which would not have been what he had envisaged. Faced with this anti-climax he did recover his amateur status for a time but by the age of 30 he had faded from the scene altogether and before long the ITA departed too and ended up bankrupt. Oh how Ian McCafferty would have thrived in the modern era!

It would seem pedantic to characterise either Lachie Stewart or Jim Alder as less talented than Ian McCafferty but perhaps even they would admit that the Law and District runner[23] had the edge when it came to comparisons at the elite world level. Lachie, of course, became a household name in Scotland after he outsprinted Ron Clarke and Dick Taylor to win the Commonwealth Games 10,000 metres title in Edinburgh in 1970. This victory was forever portrayed in the Scottish press as the unexpected triumph of a home-produced underdog denying the world's greatest ever distance runner in his final attempt to win a gold medal at a major championship.

---

[23] The Law and District Athletic Club came about in 1967 when several of the top runners from Motherwell YMCA Harriers, including Ian McCafferty, and Andy and Alex Brown, who were from the Law area, decided to form their own local club.

In fact, Lachie had been one of Britain's foremost distance runners for several years before that, competing in the steeplechase at the European Championships and Commonwealth Games in 1966 and for Britain over 10,000 metres from 1967, as well as being among the top cross country runners in Europe in the 1960s and 70s. John Caine, who ran for England in the Commonwealth race, finishing in fifth place, said that when he looked up and saw Lachie sitting in behind Taylor and Clarke, who was arguably past his best by that time, with a few laps remaining he knew the Scot would outsprint them both. Caine was no mean finisher himself but had from time to time been left trailing in the wake of the modest Shettleston Harrier.

Lachie Stewart had come up through the Scottish age groups when he competed for his home club of Vale of Leven Amateur Athletic Club from Dunbartonshire, winning the Scottish Senior Boys Cross Country Championship in 1958. He went on to win the Senior Men's title in 1967 and 1968, by now running for Shettleston, after finishing second behind Fergus Murray in 1966. He won many Scottish track titles and was AAA three mile champion in 1968. He competed for Britain at 10,000 metres in the 1972 Olympic Games in Munich after his devastating finish had ensured his selection at the British trials at Crystal Palace, nearly three quarters of a minute behind the indomitable Bedford, who won in 27:52.8. Despite the Shaftesbury Harrier's head to head with Ian McCafferty in the 5,000 metres the night before, this was a performance which had only ever been emulated by Ron Clarke and Bedford himself at that point in time. Lachie Stewart was also a popular winner of many cross country events on the continent becoming known as 'El Lachie' at Elgoibar in Northern Spain where he was a regular invitee and popular race winner.

The gregarious Jim Alder, on the other hand, would never pretend to being a finisher but was more often than not too far ahead of the field for it to make any difference. The one glaring exception was at the Scottish Cross Country Championships in Currie, Edinburgh in 1972 when his lead of 40 yards with barely a mile to go was whittled away by Ian McCafferty who, defying the heavy plough, went on to win his only Scottish Cross Country title there by six seconds.

Alder was born in Glasgow in 1940 but was a war-time orphan and was adopted by the Alder family in Morpeth after the war. Although a 'Geordie' to all intents and purposes he was very proud of his Scottish antecedents and competed for Scotland on many occasions, winning the Commonwealth marathon in Jamaica in 1966 and finishing runner up to

Ron Hill at the 1970 Games in Edinburgh in his best ever time of 2:12:04. He was also a medallist in the European Marathon Championships and in the 6 miles in Jamaica, and narrowly failed (by just 0.6 of a second) to set a UK record for the 10,000 metres in August 1965. In addition to the Scottish Senior Cross Country Championships, which Alder won three times, he and Fergus Murray played out their most intense rivalry in the Morpeth to Newcastle, competing against each other five times in this event with a final tally of four victories to one for the Morpeth Harrier on his home course. Jim Alder's world best for the two hour run on the track, of 37.994 kilometres, set at Walton-on-Thames on 17 October 1964, astonishingly, still stands today.

***

The *Scottish Athletics* yearbook for 1966 was unusually critical of Fergus Murray stating that, although he ran several fast times at three miles in 1965, 'his competitive record was not good enough for him to establish a regular place in the British team'. However, there was an underlying acceptance of his superiority in Scotland and perhaps a disappointment that, after his Olympic selection the year before, he was less to the fore in the British scene than had been expected. This seems rather harsh, given that he had improved his 5000m/three mile best and had been on the cusp of British selection throughout the season.

After his tenacious run in the East District three miles he still had time for inter-varsity events which he continued to train through or use as training runs, at the same time loyally providing his team with an invaluable competitive edge and an inspiring presence. He completed a one mile/three mile double at the Scottish Universities Championships in Aberdeen, and won the Scottish six miles title in a Scottish Native record of 28:33.4 in late June at Meadowbank, despite running in a very strong wind. At this time he was doing a lot of the Sunday training runs on the Pentlands on his own including a 2 hours 20 second clocking for his 25 mile circuit the week before his Scottish Championship win[24].

---

[24] In the days before GPS systems and 'Map My Run' apps, runners relied mostly on experience, or sometimes thread and an Ordnance Survey map, in assessing the distances they ran in training. Alistair Matson is of the view that the Sunday runs through the Pentlands were probably, given the hilly terrain involved, shorter than the distances which went into training diaries. He recalls one occasion, in April 1967, when they went 'off piste' and ended up running for 3 hours 55 minutes.

There was also a story doing the rounds at this time of the good runner and the indifferent runner going out for a training session together, the good runner recording the run in his training diary as an easy four miles and the 'scrubber', a hard five....

Fergus was based in Ilford for part of the summer and, early on, competed at venues as diverse as Minsk and Sienna. At the AAA Championships on 10 July 1965, as Ron Clarke of Australia set his iconic world record of 12:52.4 for three miles, the first sub-13 minute clocking for the distance, Fergus finished sixth in a Scottish National Record[25] of 13:21.2. However, he was not particularly happy with this run, finishing third of the British contingent behind the fast finishing Derek Graham and Bill Wilkinson after employing his favourite tactic of attempting to shake them off with three laps to go. Then, on 30 July, only three days after he had run a sub-14 minute 5,000 metres in Grosetto, he was called in at the last minute to replace Mike Wiggs (yet again) in the 5,000 metres for the Great Britain versus Poland international at the White City.

Alas, despite throwing in two 63.4 second laps three from home he was unable to sustain his effort and faded to fourth place behind Boguszewicz, who outsprinted Derek Graham, and the veteran Kazimierz Zimny, the Olympic bronze medallist from 1960, who passed him in the finishing straight. The early pace had been too slow to see off the Poles and Athletics Weekly was especially unforgiving of the home runners' performances, stating that: "The tactics called for were obvious to all.... except the two men directly involved".

The next day, with seemingly unlimited powers of recovery, Fergus easily won a three miles in an inter-club meeting for Ilford in an impressive 13:35.6 and, apparently undeterred by his poor run against Poland, which was almost certainly the result of fatigue after the trip to Grosetto, his diary reveals that 'surely I can go [close to] 20 seconds faster now'. True to his word, on 7 August, in the annual match between British Universities, the AAA and the Combined Services at Portsmouth, on the track where he had made his breakthrough two years earlier, he and a barefoot Jim Hogan pushed each other to personal bests, Murray winning by a few yards in his all-time fastest performance of 13:19.0 for three miles.

This was allegedly a 'team effort' by two stalwarts of British distance running, sharing laps and pacing each other through a 4:22 first mile, and 8:48 at two miles, until the denouement in the home straight as Murray edged home first. The plan had been for each of them to lead for two laps at a time but it was only after the race that the crafty Hogan revealed that he had devised the pace-making schedule to ensure that Murray

---

[25] This record applies to a performance by a Scottish athlete anywhere in the world. A Scottish Native record, on the other hand, can only be set by a Scottish athlete in Scotland.

was leading at the bell, giving Hogan himself a clear advantage in the last lap which he was unable to exploit. Hogan's legendary impishness was also on display at the meeting in Grosetto where he was offered a 'brown envelope' to perform the pacemaking duties in the 10,000 metres, an offer he was only too willing to accept as he would have led anyway. His reward, in lira, was the equivalent of less than £5.

Fergus's prolific racing schedule continued with victory in a two mile race on 17 August at Crystal Palace in 8:40.0 ('very disappointed not sub 8:40...') before setting out the next day for Budapest and the World Student Games in which he partnered Tim Johnston in the 5,000 metres. After a relatively straightforward heat he led for much of the way in the final on 27 August, eventually finishing third behind Sawaki of Japan and Phillip of West Germany in 13:52.6. John Keddie, in *'Scottish Athletics 1883-1983: The Official Centenary Publication of the Scottish Amateur Athletic Association'*, viewed this as perhaps Murray's best ever competitive performance in an international event. However, such an assessment pales in comparison with the mental and physical strength he displayed in maintaining such a brutal training regime, interspersed with a gruelling series of high quality races. This relentless schedule was no doubt relieved by the opportunity he and Johnston and some of the others in the British Universities team had to enjoy a break in Hungary after the championships, heading off to Lake Balaton for some sunbathing and a few runs in the surrounding hills of the Balaton Uplands National Park.

Murray resurrected his hectic programme from his Ilford base with visits to Ostrava, Pardubice, Prague and Milan for a range of races over different distances before the end of the track season, finally returning to Edinburgh University and the relative normality of the Kingsway Relays in his home town of Dundee in mid-October.

During the 1965-6 winter season, Fergus Murray was an inspirational EUHH captain and the club was finally beginning to sense that its time as the leading cross country team in Scotland was about to be realised. By now, Fergus was well known to the Scottish sporting press and reports on races often referred to his performances rather than those of the team, even when he finished down the field in order to support his less able clubmates. However, there is no doubt that his presence hugely increased the profile of the team at that time.

He ran the second fastest relay leg (to Ian McCafferty) at the Kingsway and fastest in the East District Relays in 1965, both events won easily by

EUHH. On 20 November EUHH shattered the course record in the famous Edinburgh to Glasgow Relay, winning by 80 seconds from the holders, Motherwell YMCA Harriers, with Fergus setting a groundbreaking new record of 31:07 for the seven mile sixth stage, 38 seconds faster than McCafferty and over a minute clear of Jim Alder. This record was eventually beaten by Andy McKean in 1973.

At the 'Morpeth' on 1 January 1966, in Jim Alder's absence due to injury, Fergus recorded an easy win over Lachie Stewart and Dick Taylor's elder brother Juan, going away in the final two miles to record a 'very pleasing' victory over the 13.6 mile distance in 1:05:58, which was just outside the course record. He won the Scottish Universities easily in January with the EUHH first and second teams recording sweeping victories and, after winning a road race in Sicily on 13 February, he returned two days later to Newcastle to win the British Universities Cross Country Championships by nine seconds from Mike Turner, with the Edinburgh team emulating their performance of the previous year by finishing fifth in the team race. The significance of this latter win became apparent when Turner lost the highly prestigious English Cross Country title by inches to Ron Hill four weeks later.

After yet another trip to Europe in mid-February Fergus inspired his team mates to their first ever win in the Hyde Park Relay where he almost exactly replicated his individual battle in 1964 with his perennial rival Turner, running 13:39 to the Cambridge student's 13:35. The following week, running barefoot, he all but nonchalantly won his third successive Scottish National Cross Country title by 70 yards from Lachie Stewart.

The International in Rabat in March 1966 was a huge disappointment for Murray as, hindered by the hurdles set out on the course, he trailed home in 90th place and he fared no better the following week in the annual Martini race in Brussels, complaining of having over-raced over the winter period. His erratic form continued during the early part of the track season and by the time of the mile race against McCafferty at Craiglockhart in May he was beginning to experience more problems with his knee, which was 'playing up' at about seven miles into his longer training runs. This was diagnosed by the well-disposed doctors Ian Stokoe (a former Hare and Hound himself) and Duncan McVie at the Edinburgh University Health Service as a cyst on his cartilage, the result, they surmised, of a cycling accident when he was a teenager. No X-ray was carried out. An operation was clearly necessary but, with the Commonwealth Games in mind, he decided, on his own initiative, to postpone the procedure and change his training regime to one of intensity rather than mileage. However, it meant that his original intention to go for the marathon in Kingston was no longer an option and the 3 and 6 miles became his priorities for the season. He completed his last Sunday '25' back home in Angus on 22 May and, after the East District Track Championships on 28 May, his training mileage dropped drastically in five successive weeks from 104 to a mere 40. One is left to speculate how a momentous personal decision like this for an elite athlete, in coping with serious injury, would have been dealt with in the current era.

The reduced training did not prevent him winning the Scottish Universities three miles and the Pitreavie run in early June against Ian McCafferty was an important confidence booster. It was also a virtual guarantee of selection for the Games in Kingston, Jamaica, although by this time his average weekly mileage had dropped to barely 50. Over the summer leading up to the Games he won the Scottish three mile title in a Championship record of 13:46.0 and finished ninth (fourth Briton) in the AAA race in 13:33.0 (mileage 43), behind Ron Clarke's winning time of 12:58.2. He again easily won the three miles in the British Universities v AAA v Combined Services meeting on his favourite Portsmouth track in July in 13:43.6 but he was clearly not at his best and was conscious of gradually losing fitness over the season, especially when he had to have previously unheard of days off training from time to time. Even a highly respectable two mile time of 8:41.4 behind Allan Rushmer in the Inter Area match at Birmingham on 2 July failed to stem the creeping self-doubt.

The Scottish team travelled to Kingston on 24 July but by the time of the six miles on 6 August his confidence was at a very low ebb and he finished a disappointing seventh in the hot and humid conditions in 29:40.0, and 17th in the three miles, which was held two days later, in 14:32.4. Nevertheless, he has positive memories of the friendly nature of the Games. He competed (although failed to finish due to the heat and humidity) in a pre-Games charity run at Annotto Bay on 30 July in the grounds of the local hospital and recalls hearing on the way back on the bus that England had won the World Cup.

There was little contact with the indigenous population but the large Scottish expatriate community in Jamaica provided welcome hospitality for the athletes, including invitations to barbeques and visits on yachts. Fergus was also one of a number of Scottish athletes who got into trouble with Rab Forman when, after a 'room check', they were found to have visited the women's quarters during the night, a transgression that resulted by way of atonement, and rather ironically, in additional training the next day. A 24 mile hike with Bruce Tulloh to Blue Mountain Peak, home of the famous coffee, to see the sunrise was to have been another highlight to round off the Games visit, but unfortunately they failed to realise beforehand that the mountain was covered in trees.

OXFORD DAYS

On 20 September 1966 the knee operation finally went ahead and, with a good prognosis, Murray started training again in early October. Before the end of that month, by now studying for a Dip Ed at St Catherine's College, Oxford University, his weekly mileage was back up to 70 and his training diary confirms that for the week ending 5 November he had clocked 100 miles, less than seven weeks after the operation.

The rest of the winter was spent catching up on his fitness as he approached the 1967 summer season which was to produce what he considers the best performances of his running career. While his erstwhile teammates at EUHH were enjoying unprecedented team success in Scotland, Murray found that the Oxford experience was ideal for his recovery with a relatively relaxed regime including a placement at a private school in Abingdon (which co-incidentally was Alistair Matson's *alma mater*) which offered him first class training facilities. After spending the first term in Halls, he moved to 'digs' close to the school where his landlady was the mother of the British International javelin thrower, John Fitzsimmons, a former AAA Champion.

Fergus used a one inch to the mile Ordnance Survey map to work out his training runs on the myriad of country roads in the area, based on a five mile radius from the centre of Oxford. He also trained regularly with John Waterhouse, an Oxford 'Blue', who was studying physics at the university and lived just along the road from him in Garsington. In addition to his teaching responsibilities Fergus helped with sports coaching and recalls competing in a 4 x 1 mile relay against the school team which he won after running all the legs himself.

The Bursar at 'St Cat's' at that time was Charles Wenden who also happened to be the Treasurer of the British Universities Sports Federation. He had a huge influence on the promotion of sport and encouraged top sportsmen (and later sportswomen, who were first admitted in 1974) to study at the College, which was founded in 1962. The Master of the College was the distinguished historian, Alan Bullock, who was responsible for the appointment of the Danish Modernist Architect, Arne Jacobsen, to design the new buildings. Bullock hosted a celebratory dinner at 'St Cat's' after the College won the Inter-Collegiate Sports (known as Cuppers) in 1967, with Fergus victorious in the one mile.

Serious competition gradually re-emerged into Fergus's programme with second place in a road race in Sicily in early February followed by the Hyde Park Relay (won in another record breaking time by EUHH) for St Catherine's College in the middle of the month. Here, he produced an individual leg of 14:03, after a 94 mile training week, with no tapering off for the event itself. Come 29 April he was back to his best, finishing a close second to Ron Hill in the AAA 10 mile track championships in 47:45.2, almost a minute faster than his time of three years earlier, to Hill's 47:38.0, with splits of 14:08 at three miles and 28:28 at six. However, the loose, sandy track at Hurlingham was not conducive to fast times that day and he recorded in his training diary that, on a better track, he 'felt [he] could have gone under the world record' which was held at that time by Ron Clarke at 47:12.8.

On Saturday 10 June 1967, Fergus Murray completed a week of 98 miles of running with victory in the classic Polytechnic Marathon from Windsor to Chiswick[26] in 2:19:06. It was the first event in a remarkable week of competition that saw Athletics Weekly dub the Scottish runner the 'indefatigable Fergus Murray'. This race resulted in an easy victory by nearly two minutes from Peter Yates, including unusually even splits for the normally impetuous Murray of 26:46 at 5 miles, 52:10 at ten, 78:49 at 15 and 1:44:47 at 20. Revealingly, his training diary records that, in contrast to today's events, he never took a drink and had only two 'sponge downs' throughout the entire race.

With no apparent after-effects, and feeling at the peak of his powers and full of running, he competed for a combined Oxford and Cambridge team three days later against Harvard and Yale in the two miles at the White City, winning in a meeting record of 8:44.0 following a first mile of

---

[26] The arcane marathon distance of 26 miles 385 yards, or 42.195 kilometres, was established by Polytechnic Harriers on the course from Windsor to the White City Stadium in Shepherd's Bush when it was the venue for the Olympic race in 1908, the distance of 385 yards being added to ensure that the race started from the East Terrace of Windsor Castle, to allow the royal children to watch the runners setting out, and finished in front of the Royal Box in the stadium. Previously, organisers had taken a rather cavalier attitude to the exact marathon distance and, in fact, they reverted to this approach for the 1912 and 1920 Olympic Games, before the International Amateur Athletics Federation settled, in May 1921, on the distance we know today, and adopted it for the 1924 Games in Paris.

4:16.2. However, for reasons best known to the organisers, an invitation two mile event was held separately that evening at the same venue. The television commentators were critical of the slow early pace in that race, which could have benefitted so much from Murray's input had the two races been run together, especially as it resulted in Ian McCafferty, the winner in 8:35.8, missing his own UK record by just 2.4 seconds after a much slower 4:22 first mile.

The following night in Reading, Bruce Tulloh, in his final track season, won an invitation race over the same distance in 8:35.4, with Fergus setting his best ever time of 8:38.8 in fourth place after leading for most of the way. This week of almost non-stop competition ended at Motspur Park in Surrey on Saturday 17 June with victory in the British Universities six miles in a championship record of 28:28.2, despite adverse weather conditions. He finished one minute ahead of English cross country international Roger Robinson of Cambridge University, who had been the individual winner of the British Universities Cross Country Championships earlier in the same year.

On 14 July, although his confidence had been dented by a poor run in Zurich ten days earlier, Fergus set his all-time personal best time for six miles of 27:43.2, finishing sixth in the AAA Championships behind European Champion Jürgen Haase of East Germany, the winner in 27:33.2, Lachie Stewart, who was third in 27:39.6, and Tim Johnston, fifth in 27:40.2. The illustrious quartet of Turner, Freary, Hogan and Alder trailed in behind, all in under 28 minutes in another high quality AAA race.

Fergus was then selected to run in the 10,000 metres for Britain against France in La Baule on 22 July, where he finished third behind Tim Johnston and Mike Freary, as the Britons dominated the race, and was second, behind the home favourite Lajos Mecser, for Britain against Hungary in Budapest on 29 July. The British team then travelled to Warsaw for a match against Poland on 2 August, in which he finished first equal with Lachie Stewart, again in the 10,000 metres.

Later in August he competed for Britain in the World Student Games in Tokyo but, mainly due to the heat and humidity, he was less successful this time, finishing seventh in the 10,000 metres and sixth in the 5,000 metres. This was the result of poor planning as he had gone to Tokyo with excellent credentials and plenty of confidence. However, in the 10,000 metres, where he was one of the favourites, he pushed the pace from the gun, misjudging his effort in the difficult conditions and ending up over-heating, a reaction from which he failed to recover in time for the 5,000 metres. By contrast, his fellow British distance runner John Jackson ran more judiciously and finished third in the 5,000 metres and second in the steeplechase.

Fergus's overseas adventures for the 1967 season ended with a course record in the 'Round the Bay' road race in Hamilton, Ontario on 28 October, ahead of local marathon favourite Andy Boychuk.

RETURN TO EDINBURGH

From the autumn of 1967 Murray was back in Edinburgh to take up a post at Fettes College where he taught for nearly 30 years, with a brief spell as a finance consultant and a year teaching for the local authority at Gracemount High School in the 1970s. The full time teaching job at Fettes proved rather a shock to his routine after his years as a student when he was virtually free to train and compete as much and as far afield as he liked. However, he still harboured ambitions as an athlete and he continued to train as hard as ever, although by now he realised his future lay in marathon running, and he adapted his training accordingly, with even more long runs and less in the way of *fartleks* and interval running. However, he was aware that the huge adrenalin rush he had experienced, in training and competing, from his school and early University days onwards, was beginning to fade.

Running for his new club, Edinburgh Southern Harriers, he was fastest over the long sixth stage of the Edinburgh to Glasgow Relay and won the 'Morpeth' on New Year's Day 1968 in 1:05:01, only 8 seconds outside the record set the year before by Dick Taylor. It was his only 'Morpeth' win over Jim Alder, despite the closeness of their rivalry in this event. John Caine was third, after hanging on to the leaders for most of the race, and I managed to edge clear of future Olympians Don Macgregor and Keith Angus in the run-in to finish fourth. However, indifferent form at cross country by Murray followed and his diary entry of 6 March 1968 suddenly reveals 'End. Retired from athletics. Fed up of sport and effort. [Other priorities] overtaking'. He was only 25 years old. Clearly he was burnt out from the years of relentless dedication but he was also perhaps finding the combination of a full time job, a punishing training schedule and changes in his personal circumstances, difficult to come to terms with.

It was an interlude which was to last until November of that year when, reinvigorated by the time off, he recorded that he 'missed athletics and started running again'. In the summer of 1968 he married Margaret Purvis, whom he had met at the Morningside Plaza, a local dance hall, and they lived initially in Bruntsfield and latterly in Fairmilehead in Edinburgh. Although he continued to commit wholeheartedly to the sport, and experienced a very successful 'second athletics career' as a marathon runner, the intensity of his training and his prolific racing programme had perhaps blunted his ambitions as a track runner and he never again exceeded the track times achieved in the mid-sixties.

He continued to have some success at cross country, finishing second in the 'Scottish' in 1969, and fourth in 1971, and produced his best performance, once again in bare feet, in the International Cross Country Championships on the grassy slopes at Clydebank in March 1969, finishing third of the Scottish runners (and ninth Briton) in twenty third place. During the 1969 track season he ran under 14:10 for 5,000 metres on three occasions and won the inaugural Scottish 10,000 metres title (replacing the old imperial distance of six miles) in June in 29:34.2. However, significantly, he reported in his diary, after finishing seventh in a time of 9:00 in the two miles at Edinburgh Highland Games, having led until two laps from home, that he '[didn't] seem to have real 'class' back yet!'.

His performances over the winter of 1969-70 continued to be good, if not international class, but his real focus was now on selection for the marathon at the Commonwealth Games which were to be held in Scotland for the first time, in July 1970, and perhaps a medal in the event itself. The year kicked off as usual with the 'Morpeth' (second yet again to Alder) and the Nigel Barge and then in early February he received a call out of the blue from Rab Forman asking if he would stand in at the last minute for an injured Alastair Wood to represent Britain in the Kyoto Marathon in Japan. Luckily his contract at Fettes allowed him time off for athletics and a late night call to the headmaster confirmed the go ahead[27].

Despite the extremely short notice and a long flight, it is testament to his remarkable mental strength and physical condition that Fergus finished second in a personal best of 2:18:04 behind Kokichi Uchino of Japan, after stopping at 30 kilometres to relieve a severe stitch which he feared would derail his chances in the final stages of the race. Rab Forman, who was in a following car, almost had an apoplexy.

---

[27] It was his colleagues who were affected – they had to take his classes.

49

This performance was a considerable achievement by Murray as the marathon had been for many years, and continues to be, hugely popular with the Japanese. In the 1928 and 1932 Olympics they achieved high placings in the event and the Korean runner Sohn Kee-chung (Son Kitei in Japanese) won the gold medal for Japan in Berlin in 1936, with his teammate Nam Sung-yong (Nan Shōryū) finishing third. Korea was at that time part of the Japanese Empire and Sohn was humiliated by having to represent Japan at the Games, and protested vehemently at the injustice. The national credit for the medal continued to be controversial right up until 2011 when the International Olympic Committee, while recognising Sohn's Korean background, decided to leave things as they were.

Kōkichi Tsuburaya also won a bronze medal for Japan in the 1964 Olympic race in Tokyo after entering the stadium in second place, later admitting to having been ashamed at being outsprinted by Basil Heatley of Britain in front of his home supporters. Tsuburaya committed suicide in 1968 at the Japanese Olympic training camp when he realised that injury would deprive him of the opportunity to make amends at the forthcoming Games in Mexico City. Keji Kimihara and Koichi Morishita also contributed to the Japanese marathon running dynasty by winning Olympic silver medals in 1968 and 1992 respectively.

On his return to Scotland from Japan, Murray went through the most sustained period of high mileage training in his running career in preparation for the Edinburgh Commonwealth Games, averaging over 100 miles a week for the 27 week period between mid-February and mid-August 1970, and 95 miles a week for the year as a whole. As a prelude to the Games the Scottish trial for the marathon was held over the championship course from Meadowbank Stadium to beyond Longniddry and back on 16 May, only 10 weeks before the Games themselves. The close proximity of these races would not be considered wise today especially, in Murray's case, after the marathon in Japan earlier in the year[28]. Not surprisingly for a 'home' Games there were a number of contenders for the three places in the Scottish team and, in the trial race itself, run in relatively benign conditions, a large group of runners added to the tension by staying together until the 21 mile mark, when Jim Alder made a decisive break for home, taking Murray's old rival and friend

---

[28] He also attempted a fourth marathon at the Canadian National Exhibition in Toronto on 25 August that year but dropped out at 14 miles with stomach problems. The 37 year old Alastair Wood finished second in 2:18:31, ahead of the New Zealanders Julian and Foster, and the third Scot, Pat McLagan of Victoria Park AAC, despite also being unwell, completed the distance in 2:24:34.

Donald Macgregor with him. Fergus did not appear to be at his best that day having himself attempted and failed to break clear of the field at the twenty mile mark, and rapidly becoming fatigued by his own change of pace. For a moment the fear of losing out on a Games place entered his mind but he managed to extricate himself from the remainder of the pack in the final few miles and was delighted to ensure Games selection, in third place, with something to spare.

The Games marathon itself was held on Thursday 23 July, in unusually warm and windless conditions. Although there were only 30 starters the field included some of the world's top performers at the distance including the holder of the world's best time, Derek Clayton of Australia[29], Jeff Julian of New Zealand, one of Arthur Lydiard's star 'pupils', European Champion Ron Hill, and Bill Adcocks, who had been fifth in this event at high altitude in the Mexico City Olympics two years earlier. The pace from the gun by Hill was relentless and Murray and Macgregor, who ran together for much of the race, had to apply a lot of patience and discretion in allowing the Bolton United Harrier to build up a gap of nearly two minutes over them by the ten mile mark, reached by Hill in 47:45. Clayton and Julian, who had attempted to go with Hill, surrendered to the pace but Alder and the surprising 21 year old English runner, Don Faircloth, sustained their effort and were hauled to personal bests behind Hill's winning time of 2:09:28[30]. Fergus worked his way slowly through the field to seventh place but he was disappointed with his run despite it being a significant personal best of 2:15:32, only 22 seconds behind Adcocks, with Macgregor eighth in 2:16:53.

After years of steady improvement throughout the 1960s, Donald Macgregor's own career was beginning to take off at this time, despite his being three years older than Murray. After coming in third (second Briton) in the Maxol Marathon in Manchester in June 1972, he was selected to run for Britain in the Olympic Games in Munich where he finished seventh, one place behind the British 'Number 1', Ron Hill. Hill

---

[29] The Cumbria-born Clayton was the first man to break 2:10 for the marathon at Fukuoka, Japan in December 1967, but his subsequent time of 2:08:33.6, set at Antwerp in May 1969, only 11 days after a 2:17:26 marathon in Turkey, proved controversial because there were question marks about the exact measurement of the course.

[30] This time was subsequently considered by some, although not by Hill himself, as the world record for the distance due to the issues surrounding Clayton's run at Antwerp.

had been one of the favourites to win the Olympic title and his failure to live up to expectations is often put down to his carbohydrate diet being upset by the one day delay to the event resulting from the terrorist attack on the Israeli team quarters. However, Macgregor's view is that Hill, who had been undergoing altitude training in St Moritz with the British distance running squad, came down from altitude several days after the other runners which was too late to allow his body to reacclimatise at the lower level[31].

Although originally from Edinburgh, Donald Macgregor eventually settled in St Andrews, where he had been a student and a leading member of the athletics and cross country teams in the 1950s and 60s, and was later a Liberal Democrat Councillor and well-known figure in the town. He set his best time of 2:14:15.4 for the marathon at the Commonwealth Games in Christchurch, New Zealand in January 1974, where he finished sixth.

After finishing second in a half marathon in Puerto Rico in February 1971, Murray teamed up with Macgregor once again for Britain in the classic marathon run over the 1896 Olympic course (reprised for the 2004 Games) from Marathon to Athens, in April 1971. This course and the history of the event are described in detail by Donald Macgregor in his autobiography published in 2010[32]. A headwind slowed the winner, Usami of Japan, that day by approximately 8 minutes to 2:19:25, with

---

[31] Ron Hill was instrumental in the popularising of the carbohydrate loading diet in the late 1960s which helped runners overcome carbo depletion in the latter stages of the marathon. The diet involved a long run on the Sunday before the race, and then starving the body of carbohydrate for a few days, before reversing the intake in the final three days before competition. It was what London Marathon Director and 1956 Olympic Steeplechase Gold Medallist Chris Brasher referred to in his 'Observer' column as an 'overloading phenomenon' and led to events such as the 'pasta party' which was held on the eve of the London Marathon each year. Nowadays, elite runners get round the problem with a more measured approach to diet before competition and by consuming carbohydrate gels during the event itself, thus avoiding the negative aspects of the original diet which could upset metabolism and cause a demoralising bloating effect for athletes going into a race. Hill was also responsible for other innovations such as the use of synthetic materials in running kit, which were less likely to retain moisture, and the mesh running vest and reflective 'silver' shorts which were designed to reduce the possibility of over-heating, particularly in long distance events in hot climates. His background in textiles from his doctorate at Manchester University eventually led to him running a highly successful sports clothing company, Ron Hill Sports, which diversified and continues to trade successfully today under new management.

[32] 'Running My Life', published by Pinetree Press.

Murray fourth in 2:25:05 and Macgregor fifth in 2:26:02.

Fergus Murray's final race at international level was the Maxol Marathon (scene of Macgregor's success the following year) in June 1971 when he was picked for a British team to compete against West Germany. He made the mistake of driving down the day before and, feeling out of sorts early in the race, decided to drop out after only 8 miles, and returned home the same day.

Although Fergus was still capable of running 5,000 metres in under 14 minutes, and achieved this for the last time in winning the East District Championships in May 1973 (with 13:59.6), his performance levels gradually began to wane. Interestingly, however, his 14:07.0 timing in finishing second to Bernie Plain in a British League club match at Meadowbank early in the summer of 1974 did re-ignite his ambitions for a brief period and gave him hope 'for sub-13:45 this season', which would have been a personal best, but which sadly did not materialise.

He had started to accept by the early 1970s that his performances were not going to improve if he was going to have to reconcile a serious teaching job with serious athletics, a combination he found just too demanding. His athletics ambitions and an ongoing feeling of unfinished business in the sport were, he feels, to blame for one or two bad moves in his life. A significant one was his decision to leave Fettes after six years in 1973 to work for Anthony Gibbs in the financial sector which he initially found very stimulating and which offered him the chance to exploit his nous in this field.

The move into finance also renewed his hunger for athletics for a time but difficulties in the industry in 1974 resulted in him being made redundant less than a year after his appointment. Luckily, he was able to secure the post teaching chemistry for the local authority at Gracemount and, although teacher unrest over contracts in the public sector was beginning to take hold, he enjoyed the year, particularly the social life and the co-educational environment. However, after reassessing his priorities, he was given the opportunity to resume teaching at Fettes, finally giving up on his aspirations for financial success and indeed, and at long last, for serious competitive athletics, to concentrate on his teaching career.

REFELECTIONS ON THE MURRAY ERA

Apart from the relentless training and the races at venues in parts of the world as diverse as South America, Canada, North Africa, Japan and many European countries, Fergus Murray lived a simple life during his running career, particularly as a student. In his first year at university he stayed for a few weeks in Joppa but it was too far away from his department at King's Buildings and the running environs of the Pentlands, The Meadows and the Braid Hills and he moved to 'digs' in Mayfield Terrace on the south side of Edinburgh where he was looked after for four years by his landladies, Ena and Molly Cameron. Chris Elson was also a boarder, later on Ian Young and I spent some time there, and Alistair Matson, Roger Young and the Wight brothers lived nearby.

In 1965 he moved to a rented house in Morningside which he shared for three years with five of his EUHH team mates. Everyone had his own room and organised his own cooking (herring and potatoes or cheap cuts of meat) in the large communal kitchen which provided the only regular source of heat (the cooker) in the house. If someone was especially hungry there was a chip shop down the road and lunches at the Refectory or the Student Union often provided the main meal of the day.

Diets or vitamins were never mentioned and drug use never extended beyond 'Dextrosol' or a milky 'Nescafé'. The house became known amongst the running fraternity as 'The Zoo' where 'The Beast', 'The Bear' and 'The Bomb' lived and 'The Crab' (Martin Craven) occasionally came to visit, although there was no mention at that time of a 'Baby Bear'. The writer and journalist John Bryant who was an Oxford 'Blue' in the steeplechase, was a resident of 'The Zoo' in 1966-67 (after Fergus Murray had left for Oxford) while he was working in Edinburgh for the Evening News.[33]

Training was very serious and, to save money, bath water was shared (although never at exactly the same time), but parties were numerous and unusually civilised, perhaps even a little *passé*, for the 'swinging sixties'. A training chart logging the weekly mileage was displayed on the kitchen wall, with a total target of 600 miles. There was an apocryphal tale that one of the less serious runners came home on a Saturday night

---

[33] In extremely controversial circumstances, when he was with the Daily Mail in the 1980s, John Bryant was involved in the newspaper persuading Zola Budd's father to encourage her to apply for British citizenship on the grounds that her grandfather was British, thus circumventing the international sporting boycott of South Africa and allowing her to compete in the 1984 Summer Olympics in Los Angeles.

and wrote 20 miles on the chart, giving the house a total for the week of 598 miles. He was immediately ordered out for another two miles before midnight. Tellingly, the 'Zoo' years coincided almost exactly with the main team successes of EUHH from 1965 to 1968.

Fergus, as a successful British international runner, was provided with free shoes by Puma, obtaining them direct from Rudolph Dassler in Germany, rather than through the UK representative who was Derek Ibbotson. Another major 'star' of British athletics, the 400m runner Robbie Brightwell, who was captain of the British athletics team at the Tokyo Olympics, was the representative in the UK at the time for Puma's bitter rival Adidas, which was founded and run by Rudolph's estranged younger brother Adolph. Puma developed lightweight road racing shoes but Murray, who rarely wore socks for racing or training, found these uncomfortable, and used them sparingly, often reverting to Tiger 'Cubs', thin soled canvas road shoes made in Japan by Onitsuka[34], which were very popular with distance runners in the 1960s. As an amateur athlete Murray was not compelled to wear Puma shoes in all his races but obviously he had an obligation to use them as much as possible, especially in high profile events. He often trained in 'Tigers' but other runners mainly used them only for racing as, at that time, in the early stages of running shoe technology, they offered insufficient protection against the pounding of weekly mileage which could lead to long term injuries to the knees or shins.

Kit otherwise was basic, restrained and free of branding – cotton shorts, running vests and T shirts in the summer, long sleeved cotton tops and woollen tracksuits in the winter. The official EUHH club colours of plain green vests and white shorts were very low key compared with other clubs like Strathclyde University or Dundee Hawkhill – even Glasgow University stretched to two colours on their vests, black and gold. For the sake of decorum, jock straps (most commonly 'Litesome') were referred to as 'athletic supports' when ordered over the counter at sports shops. The ridiculous but irresistibly comfortable 'freedom' shorts, which failed miserably in the fashion stakes, became popular in the 1970s and older runners jest that they are eternally grateful to have missed out on the mercilessly revealing Lycra leggings and tops of the present day.

---

[34] The company was formed by Kihachiro Onitsuka in 1949 with the intention of raising post-war youth self-esteem in Japan through athletics, and continues to this day through its parent company ASICS. Abebe Bikila was allegedly persuaded to try out Tiger 'Cubs' in the 1950s, instead of running in bare feet, although he successfully defended his Olympic marathon title in 1964 wearing Puma shoes.

Despite all his successes at international level, and the fact that track running was his *raison d'être*, Fergus Murray's main enjoyment in the sport was as part of a team, competing for his club, whether it was Dundee Hawkhill or Edinburgh Southern or Ilford or Edinburgh University Hare and Hounds, in road relays or cross country team events. The early battles with the often unfairly underrated Craig Douglas and the Teviotdale Harriers club in East of Scotland cross country events bring back fond memories. As an individual his main goal always focussed on improvement and any elation he experienced was from personal best times and not from wins over the likes of Mel Batty, in the Leyton Floodlight meeting in 1964, or Bruce Tulloh, in Finland in the same year. They were his heroes and disrespect for his peers just wasn't in his make up.

It was with mixed feelings that the modest, unassuming but engaging Fergus Murray, by then on his Dip Ed course at St Catherine's College, Oxford, came to Parliament Hill Fields in February 1967 to see his great legacy fulfilled. Unable to compete himself due to a late flight back from the race in Sicily, he watched his 'pupils' from EUHH win the British Universities Cross Country Championships for only the second time in the Club's history, a feat which 50 years later has only once been emulated in the men's team event by a Scottish University (Glasgow University, in 1984). It begs the question whether Oxford University would have won that day if Murray had competed for them, but the answer is a resounding 'No'. Despite his pedigree the winning margin was just too great.

56

Fergus Murray (l) competing at Caird Park for Dundee Hawkhill Harriers in the early 1960s.
(from collection of Fergus Murray, photographer unknown)

Fergus Murray emulates Elliott and Cerutty on the dunes at Monifieth in the 1960s.
(Alistair Barrie)

EUHH teammates Roger Young (l), Fergus Murray and Martin Craven at Craiglockhart Playing Fields in the summer of 1963. The old timber pavilion can be seen in the background.
(from collection of Fergus Murray, photographer unknown)

Allan Faulds (Glasgow) leads from Donald Macgregor (St Andrews), Martin Craven (Edinburgh), the eventual winner, and Fergus Murray (Edinburgh) in the three miles at the Scottish Universities Championships, Westerlands, Glasgow, June 1963.
(from collection of Allan Faulds, photographer unknown)

1962 Commonwealth and European Marathon Champion Brian Kilby (Coventry Godiva) leads the field in the 1964 Morpeth to Newcastle Road Race from eventual winner, John Anderson (Saltwell), Jim Alder (Morpeth) and Fergus Murray (Dundee Hawkhill). (Newcastle Chronicle and Journal Limited, photographer unknown, from collection of Fergus Murray)

Mike Turner (l) and Fergus Murray run in together in the British Universities Cross Country Championships in Nottingham, February 1964. (The Times, photographer unknown, from collection of Fergus Murray)

Mel Batty leads from Fergus Murray in the AAA 10 mile championships at Hurlingham in April 1964. Batty won in a world record time of 47:26.8. Murray achieved the Olympic qualifying time for 10,000 metres *en route* and was subsequently picked for the Olympic Games in Tokyo later that year.
(from collection of Fergus Murray, photographer unknown)

Press cutting from a Finnish newspaper showing Fergus Murray winning the 5,000 metres from Bruce Tulloh in the match against Finland in Helsinki, July 1964.
(from collection of Fergus Murray, photographer unknown)

Model of the Olympic Stadium in Helsinki presented to Fergus Murray in recognition of the track record he set for 5,000 metres in the match against Finland, July 1964. (Alison Blamire)

Gerry Lindgren (USA) leads from Ron Clarke (Australia) in the AAA three miles at the White City in July 1965. Clark won in a world record time of 12:52.4, the first sub-13 minute clocking for the distance. Mike Wiggs is lying third and barefoot Bruce Tulloh fourth. Fergus Murray (number 22) set a Scottish national record of 13:21.2 in sixth place. (Daily Mirror, photographer unknown, from collection of Fergus Murray)

Mike Turner and Ron Hill battle out the final strides of the English National Cross Country Championships in March 1966, which Hill won by inches. In February that year Fergus Murray defeated Turner in the British Universities Championships in Newcastle. (Ed Lacey/Popperfoto/Getty Images)

Fergus Murray (15) in a group of runners at the Kyoto Marathon, February 1970. He finished second in a personal best of 2:18:04, despite only having a few days' notice of the race.
(from collection of Fergus Murray, photographer unknown)

X

Ian Stewart holds off Ian McCafferty in the final of the 5,000 metres at the Commonwealth Games, Edinburgh in July 1970. Kip Keino of Kenya is in the background.
(Ed Lacey/Popperfoto/Getty Images)

Craig Douglas hands over to Fergus Murray for Edinburgh Southern Harriers at the end of the first stage of the Edinburgh to Glasgow Relay in November 1970. Number Z1 is Hugh Barrow of Victoria Park AAC. Shettleston Harriers won the race from Edinburgh Southern, with Victoria Park third.
(with kind permission of The Scotsman Publications Ltd, photographer Denis Straughan)

Fergus Murray (Edinburgh Southern) and Dick Wedlock (Shettleston) battle out the second leg of the Edinburgh to Glasgow Relay in November 1970 with Lachie Stewart, who won the Commonwealth 10,000 metres from Ron Clarke earlier that year, looking on. Wedlock ran the fastest leg, with Murray one second behind.
(with kind permission of The Scotsman Publications Ltd, photographer Denis Straughan)

Chapter 3:

THE EUHH TEAM OF THE 1960s

The Edinburgh University Hare and Hounds club was founded in 1890[35] and competed in inter-club events in addition to University fixtures. It was one of the main teams in the East of Scotland in the first half of the 20th century. Although the Club was kept active during the years of World War Two, it was in the immediate post-war period that it began to expand, with many ex-servicemen joining the Club in pursuit of exercise to accompany their studies. The team was especially successful in the late 1940s, winning the Scottish Universities, the East District Championships and bronze at the British Universities in season 1948-49. In 1949-50 they won the British Universities team title for the first time, a major achievement, and went on in the 1950s to win the Scottish Junior team race five times, the East Districts six times, and to complete eleven successive Scottish Universities team victories.

THE EARLY 1960s

Much of the success of the team at this time coincided with the presence of Adrian Jackson, from Leeds, who studied medicine at Edinburgh from 1953 to 1960. He was a prolific winner of races in the east of Scotland and at University and Scottish national level, and his athletics career almost appears a precursor of Fergus Murray's. Among Jackson's successes were the Scottish Universities Cross Country, mile and three mile titles, the East District cross country, mile and three mile titles, and the Scottish National mile and three mile titles, and he set a number of championship records on the track. His finest achievements were outstanding individual victories in the British Universities Cross Country Championships in 1955 and 1957, the British Universities 3 miles in 1955 and the World Student Games 5,000 metres in San Sebastian in the same year. His 14:13.6 clocking for 5,000 metres at an international meeting in Helsinki in 1956 was 10th on the British all-time rankings at that time. While still a student, and qualifying on residency grounds, he competed for Scotland in the International Cross Country Championships in 1958 (finishing 46th) and 1960 (30th).

After graduating in 1960 Jackson stayed on in Edinburgh as a member

---

[35] An Edinburgh University Harriers Club also existed between 1874 and 1887.

of Braidburn Athletic Club, winning the East District cross country title for a fourth time in 1961, finishing sixth in the Scottish National, and competing for a third time (finishing 51st) for Scotland in the International Cross Country Championships which were held in Nantes, France, that year. Adrian then concentrated on his medical career, becoming a consultant anaesthetist at Cheltenham General Hospital. However, while at Cheltenham he rejoined his old club, Leeds St Marks, and finished a creditable 29th in the English Cross Country Championships in March 1962. He made a comeback as a veteran athlete in the 1980s winning 15 gold medals at the World Medical Games and latterly ran the London Marathon.

Following Jackson's graduation the team went through a less successful, less dedicated period, despite the efforts of the likes of Doug Dingwall and Barry Stacey and, in particular, Martin Craven from Kendal. Martin developed into one of the leading runners in Scotland at the time, finishing fifth in the Scottish National Senior Cross Country Championships in 1963 and gaining a Scottish 'vest' in the International Cross Country Championships in San Sebastian that year. In 1960-61 the EUHH team was third in the East Districts, first in the Scottish Universities and third in the Scottish National Junior Championships, although no significant individual performances were recorded.

Glasgow University Hares and Hounds were the main rivals in University competition in the early 1960s with their leading runners Doug Gifford, Calum Laing, Jim Bogan and Allan Faulds[36]. Meanwhile, following successful seasons by Shettleston Harriers and Edinburgh Southern Harriers, Motherwell YMCA Harriers were beginning to emerge as the dominant road and cross country running team on the club front led by Andy Brown, Bert McKay, Dave Simpson, John Linaker, a belated recruit from Pitreavie Athletic Club in Fife, and, in due course, Andy Brown's younger brother Alex, and Ian McCafferty.

It was with the arrival of Fergus Murray and Chris Elson in 1961 that the seeds of later EUHH success were planted. Although weekly mileages were much lower than in later years, training became more regimented with the introduction of *fartleks* and repetition hill runs on the grassy slopes of Holyrood Park during the week and regular team runs of seven

---

[36] The Glasgow team was managed in the 1950s and 60s by Willie Diverty who, among other roles, was the Scottish correspondent for Athletics Weekly for many years. Willie was very popular with runners and officials, including the EUHH team, and was President of the Scottish Cross Country Union when it hosted the International Championships at Clydebank in 1969.

to 10 miles steady each Sunday. Alex Wight had come to Edinburgh from Berwickshire High School a year earlier, and was a mainstay of the EUHH second team at first, but the forward-looking approach to training which Elson in particular was espousing, combined with Murray's determined mindset, must have convinced him about the benefits of dedicated training which he was able to exploit so successfully after his early student days.

Nevertheless, marked progress by EUHH in competition was not apparent at first and over the 1961-62 season the only minor success for the team was second place, to Glasgow, in the Scottish Universities, with first-year student Elson leading them home in fourth place. Elson was also first counter, in 10th place, for the Junior team which was fourth in the Scottish National Championships, but the only other individual performance of any significance was Murray's 14:17 leg in the Hyde Park Relay.

In season 1962-63 the team finished eighth in the Edinburgh to Glasgow but, with Roger Young and Gareth Evans among the newcomers (together with Jim Wight, who would make an impact later on), they improved significantly over the latter part of the winter season, finishing second in the East Districts (with Elson second in the individual race) and winning the Scottish Universities (with Craven second and Elson third) and Scottish National Junior team titles (Murray first). At the British Universities, despite Murray's absence due to illness, the team was a creditable seventh and, individually, Craven, Murray and Elson (the latter two only 20 years of age) were among the top runners in the country.

THE MID 1960s

Further progress was made in 1963-64 when the club was awarded the special set of medals in the Edinburgh to Glasgow Relay as the most improved team, in fifth place. This was the result of consistent, if unremarkable, running by team members bolstered by the stellar contribution of Murray who ran the fastest second leg, taking the team briefly into third place. The other individual performances in the event ranged between Young, who was fifth fastest on the tough sixth stage, to Grant, 13th fastest on stage eight. The team's best performance after Christmas that season was in the Scottish National Junior when they again secured the title with excellent 'packing' between the talented half milers, Dave Orr, in 10th place, and Gareth Evans, in 14th. Jim Wight and

Frank Gamwell were the other counting runners.

In the meantime, Fergus Murray won the first of his three successive National Senior individual titles running for his home club, Dundee Hawkhill Harriers, who finished sixth in the team race. However, despite Murray's superb performances in the British Universities, where he finished first equal with Mike Turner, and the Hyde Park, where he ran the second fastest leg, the team failed in both cases to take advantage of his exceptional individual running, finishing 11th and ninth respectively.

Ian Young and I were among the student intake in 1964 and we both went into the first team at the first time of asking. We were from that pool of runners who had the advantage of a background of competition at the national junior level before coming to university. This was especially so in the case of Young who had had considerable success as a youth and junior running for Springburn Harriers, in the company of Eddie Knox and Duncan Middleton who were among the top runners in Britain in their age group. He also competed for the Scottish Junior team in the International Cross Country Union Championships in Dublin, where he finished 22nd.

In the Edinburgh to Glasgow in 1964, I finished fourth on Stage 1 and Ian Young was fastest on Stage 8. Between us no individual EUHH runners were outside the top five on their stages, with Murray fastest on Stage 2 and Elson second fastest on Stage 5. However, Motherwell YMCA, bolstered by the addition of Dick Wedlock, who had transferred, temporarily as it transpired, from Shettleston Harriers, were still dominant in Scotland, winning for the third time in a row and finishing over two minutes clear as EUHH achieved the highest ever placing by a university team at that time, in second place.

With Roger Young a natural and inspiring captain, EUHH continued to progress throughout 1964-65, winning the East Districts (with Murray and Roger Young first and second in the individual race), the Scottish Universities (with Murray first and Elson third), and the Scottish National Junior (with Roger Young second and Ian Young sixth). Despite having to spread resources between the two age groups the EUHH team were also third in the Scottish National Senior race and performed well in the British Universities in Nottingham, finishing fifth, with Murray second individual behind Mike Turner, in the same time, after a brutal encounter of the highest international class, with the lead changing hands several times throughout the race.

However, 1965-66 was the season that EUHH finally broke through into number one spot in Scotland. Fergus Murray was captain for the season and Gareth Bryan-Jones and Dave Logue arrived from Leeds University and Belfast respectively to bolster the 'old guard' of Murray, the Wight brothers, Roger Young and Elson, Gamwell, Evans, Allan and Matson and the 'young pretenders' Ian Young and me. Murray produced a small booklet which outlined training schedules and advice on competition, diet and kit for freshman athletes, which I replicated the following year[37].

Many of the EUHH team lived in the south side of Edinburgh and often met up for an evening *fartlek* session. The Club's official training session together was held every Wednesday afternoon at King's Buildings, the University's science campus to the south of the city[38]. After a friendly address from the captain about the race on the coming Saturday, and any forthcoming social events such as the 'Harriers Hop', runners were split into 'packs' – slow, medium and fast – with the fast pack engaging in a 10 mile *fartlek* on the nearby roads, fields and tracks which, although never intended to be competitive, nevertheless allowed athletes to stretch each other and perhaps indulge in a degree of gamesmanship in the long strides on the Braid Hills or down 'The Hermitage' back to King's Buildings. The advantage of the 'packs' was that you never had to train above or below your own level and highly experienced runners such as Chris Lord and Brian Covell were always on hand to guide newcomers through the nuances, and indeed decorum, of a team training session. After training, team members were able to enjoy a snack together in the canteen at 'KB', and the committee, made up of the Captain, Vice-Captain, Secretary, Assistant Secretary and Treasurer, met to pick the teams for the Saturday races and to write up previous results.

Several dedicated members of the team also met up at King's Buildings on Sunday mornings to do a long run on the nearby Pentland Hills to the south of Edinburgh. However, in the autumn of 1965 Alistair Matson secured the lease, eventually extended to three years, of the detached

---

[37] Following distribution of the booklet in 1966-67, I was accused by one of the younger athletes of expecting him to cover 100 miles a week in training. Although patently not the case, this misunderstanding underlines the attitude to training which prevailed with the EUHH team at that time.

[38] It was a tradition at Edinburgh, and other universities, in the interests of a holistic education, for Wednesday afternoons to be reserved for non-academic pursuits, particularly sport, although some of the newer, less traditional departments, including architecture, eschewed the notion.

house at 78 Morningside Drive, in the leafy environs of South Edinburgh, which became known as 'The Zoo'. With equally easy access to the Pentlands it took over as the meeting point for the 'Sunday 21' which set out via Glenlockhart and Colinton Dell, and on to Currie and Balerno before heading into the Pentlands past Threipmuir reservoir and Bavelaw Castle. The trail then passed through the 'Green Cleuch' to the paved road which took them east past Loganlee and Glencorse reservoirs to Flotterstone, where they turned left on to the main Biggar Road to Fairmilehead, and back down the long incline to Morningside.

On occasion the run was executed in the opposite direction, with perhaps an extra loop added on to take the overall distance to 25 miles. Aside from the residents of 'The Zoo' others such as Sandy Cameron, Jim Wight and, if he was in town, Donald Macgregor, would join the party. Fergus Murray, as the most accomplished of the runners, was always on hand to ensure, in his even-handed way, that no-one who was feeling 'good' on a particular Sunday got carried away and started to push the pace into racing mode. The plan was always to finish the run together – there were plenty of opportunities to 'do your own thing' on other occasions.

The Meadows was also, and indeed still is, an extremely popular training venue which offered the option of off-road training on grass or tarmac paths, with the added bonus of being floodlit by street lamps in winter. Here, a lap of one and three quarter miles could be devised through the best use of the lighting, and Bruntsfield Links to the south west could be added to give a lap of two and a half miles or so. Holyrood Park was another favourite, with its hill training possibilities, and Peffermill playing fields and Inverleith Park next to the Botanical Gardens, although more detached from student territory, were well used for interval and *fartlek* sessions, or steady runs of laps on grass. For those who favoured track training, Meadowbank Stadium and Saughton Enclosure, and Craiglockhart, once the rugby season was over and the track marked up, were the main options for students in the city.

In November 1965 all the EUHH effort in training paid off handsomely with a sweeping victory in the Edinburgh to Glasgow Relay. This was achieved despite the absence through injury of newcomer Gareth Bryan-Jones and the team's winning time shattered the course record by 7 minutes 15 seconds, the largest single improvement in the 72 year history of the event, with the holders, Motherwell YMCA, Victoria Park AAC and Edinburgh Southern Harriers also within the previous fastest time. Four of the EUHH team were fastest on their legs and on only a single leg was the EUHH team outside the top three individual times. After a fierce battle with Ian Binnie of Victoria Park, who had mysteriously re-emerged, at the age of 38, to compete in the event for the first time in four years, I managed to set a new record on the first stage and Fergus Murray and Jim Wight set new records on the sixth and seventh stages.

The team effortlessly won every significant event in Scotland that season including the East District Relays, the East Districts, the Scottish Universities and the Scottish National Senior Championships (where their six counting runners finished in the first 21 finishers with Fergus Murray victorious, Roger Young eighth and Dave Orr tenth), and were third in the Scottish National Junior (with me third and Jim Wight sixth) on the same day. The Scottish Universities result included another astonishing statistic to rival the Edinburgh to Glasgow success as EUHH runners filled eight of the first nine places in the first team race (the perennial interloper, in second place, being Bill Ewing of Aberdeen University, who was one of the very few athletes from another university at that time who would have been good enough to 'walk' into the EUHH team) and the first eight in the second team race held on the same day in Aberdeen.

EUHH also won the Hyde Park Relay for the first time, setting a new course record of 85:52, averaging 14:19 for each of the six legs of approximately three miles. Murray was second fastest overall with 13:39 in bringing the team home on the final leg, over a minute clear of Borough Road College, and the night of celebration at the Metric lasted until the final Tube run back to Ilford where most of the team were staying.

EUHH were now on the crest of a wave of ascendancy in Scotland but were still unable to crack the conundrum of the British Universities Championships where the team finished a disappointing fifth at Newcastle despite Murray's resounding individual victory over Mike Turner. But how lucky were students compared with some of the opposition in Scotland, many of whom worked on Saturday mornings before competition. One of the most successful athletes in the Motherwell YMCA Harriers club, which was the top team in Scotland immediately before EUHH, was Davie Simpson who rivalled even Alf Tupper by allegedly working a shift in the pits before competing in the afternoon. Gordon Eadie of Cambuslang, a prominent marathon runner, was a coalman who delivered on Saturday mornings and often turned up at races with his face still smeared with coal dust masquerading as mascara, no doubt fatigued from shifting sacks of coal around all morning.

Consider too the disadvantages Scottish club athletes had over the summer season having to cope with indifferent weather and poor tracks at the ubiquitous Highland Games where well-meant but bizarre prizes such as pedestal ash trays and candlewick bedspreads were on offer to the winners[39]. Runners such as Andy and Alex Brown and John Linaker would have had even more impressive times had more opportunities for regular competition in the south been on offer but the costs of travel and time off would have prohibitive for all but the most fortunate.

The Edinburgh students had the benefit of free travel[40] to events in England and Northern Ireland, as well as Scotland, including inter-university matches in Leeds, Belfast and Newcastle, the British Universities Championships and Hyde Park Relay and, in the summer, the Durham Trophy meeting and the British Universities Track Championships. Here, competition, often against top British athletes such as Ron Hill, Tim Johnston, Mike Turner, Andy Holden and Frank Briscoe (and, indeed, Fergus Murray himself), would change perspectives for the more ambitious EUHH runners. In addition, the athletics team from time to time organised tours abroad in the summer, for example to Scandinavia (in 1967) and Ireland (1969), again with some financial assistance from the university.

THE PEAK YEAR AND BEYOND

In 1966-67 EUHH were so dominant in Scotland by the time of the Edinburgh to Glasgow Relay in November that, as captain this time, I somehow didn't seem to consider it either arrogant or presumptuous when hastily scribbling down a victory speech on the bus after handing over in the lead at the end of the first leg of the race. The gist of the short

---

[39] There is an apocryphal tale of a leading runner slowing down at the end of a road race in order to win the transistor radio for finishing second, rather than the alabaster table lamp which was on offer to the winner.

[40] At Edinburgh University in the 1960s, sport was funded through a compulsory 'composite fee' paid by every student on matriculation. It was additional to tuition fees and the funds generated were then dispersed to the various student groups including the unions, the athletic clubs and student societies. The allocation of funds was done by a Composite Fee Disbursement Committee chaired by Lord Cameron, who was the Chancellor's Assessor at the time, and a High Court Judge. Cash was never handled by students and club officials usually made the travelling and accommodation arrangements through a travel agent who then invoiced the Edinburgh University Athletic Club [now the Edinburgh University Sports Union] every month. A similar arrangement exists today but there is less funding allocated through fees and more in the way of sponsorship, club membership fees and fundraising.

spiel, delivered in a quivering voice at the famous Ca'd'Oro Restaurant, where the generous sponsorship of the *'News of the World'* extended to a free meal for all the competitors and officials after the race[41], was a parody on the constant reports in the press that EUHH now won races 'despite the absence of A F Murray'. It claimed, with tongue in cheek, that EUHH won 'because of the absence of A F Murray', Fergus having left for Oxford a few months earlier.

The 1966 Edinburgh to Glasgow victory was achieved in a time only 21 seconds outside EUHH's own record but with a much greater winning margin of 3 minutes 42 seconds (over Victoria Park AAC). This was the result of record times on individual legs by me, Hathorn and Elson on the first, third and eighth legs respectively, fastest time on the seventh leg by Jim Wight, and equally meritorious performances on all of the other legs as the team of green-vested students led all the way from Iain Hathorn's third stage run through Uphall in West Lothian, to the finish over 30 miles away in Glasgow's Ingram Street. Colin Shields (in *'Runs Will Take Place, Whatever the Weather: The Centenary History of the Scottish Cross Country Union 1890-1990'*) wrote that 'The students ran as if they knew they would win, never looking round at their pursuing rivals, their sole aim the next changeover point, and displaying a zealous professionalism [sic] in the best sense of the word'.

In January 1967 EUHH had the honour of being invited, thanks to the guidance of Kenny Ballantyne of Edinburgh Southern Harriers, who had competed there in 1966, to represent Scotland, as national cross country champions, in the European Clubs Cross Country Championships in Arlon in Belgium. The competition over a muddy course of laps did not suit everyone but, led home by Ian Young, EUHH finished a creditable fifth in the team race which was won by the English Champions, City of Stoke. Gaston Roelants, the Olympic Steeplechase Champion from Belgium, was first in the individual race, ahead of Stoke's English Internationalists Roy Fowler and John Jackson.

The evening afterwards was equally memorable as teams let off the steam which had no doubt built up over weeks of preparation and training. There is a rumour that the marks still evident on the walls of a nondescript hostelry in Arlon in the foreign fields of south east Belgium, on the border with Luxembourg, were caused by students in the 1960s

---

[41] In addition to the Edinburgh to Glasgow, the 'News of the World' sponsored the equivalent event in England, the London to Brighton Road Relay, and many international track and field meetings in the UK in the 1950s and 60s.

throwing mud pies at the windows in order to attract attention after being locked out for the night. Despite the shenanigans, EUHH were invited back to this event, again as Scottish Champions, in 1969.

In the meantime, back in Scotland, the remainder of the EUHH team still managed to finish second in the East District Championships with Dave Logue, who had been unable to travel to Arlon, a fine third in the individual race. The following week EUHH exceeded their performance of the year before in the Scottish Universities Championships, held over their home course from 'KB', with their complement of eight runners finishing ahead of all the athletes from the other universities in Scotland, Bill Ewing having graduated by then. The eight were selected to represent Scottish Universities against the Universities Athletic Union (the body responsible for English and Welsh Universities, with the exception of Oxford, Cambridge and London) in a representative match to be held in conjunction with the following week's British Universities Championships at Parliament Hill Fields in London. However, the EUHH committee decided to select Chris Elson, who won the second team race in a time which would have been good enough for fifth place in the first team race, resulting in the unique situation of EUHH having nine runners in the British Universities event, with Willie Allan good enough to represent Scottish Universities but not quite good enough for EUHH.

At the British Universities on 5 February at Parliament Hill Fields in London the team finally came good with team victory on 87 points, from Cambridge University on 113 points, London 126 and Oxford 140, well ahead of the leading English 'provincial' team from Leeds University who finished on 294. The individual race was won in 30:26 by Roger Robinson of Cambridge University, an English Cross Country International, with Ian Young leading EUHH home in eighth place in 31:11 ahead of Jim Wight, 11th in 31:25, Gareth Bryan-Jones, 13th in 31:36, me, 14th in 31:37, Alex Wight, 20th in 31:52, and Chris Elson, 21st in 31:53. Dave Logue was 23rd in 31:58, and Iain Hathorn (despite suffering from whooping cough) finished a gutsy 49th in 33:01 to complete the Edinburgh team. It was a triumph of teamwork by a club without, at least at that time, any 'star' individual performers. Willie Allan, running for Scottish Universities, finished 34th in 32:24 with the UAU narrowly defeating the EUHH/Scottish Universities team in the parallel event.

Fifty years later, I recall that: *'We travelled down by air on the Friday evening. Dave Logue and I stayed with Frank Gamwell's aunt and uncle in the Woodford area. Frank and his pals from Ilford Athletic Club were heroes and great supporters that day. The race itself was very intense and, because the EUHH runners were all of a similar standard, with no stars at that point, several of us almost coincidentally ran as a group for most of the race. Near the end Gareth shouted to me that our places were being threatened by rising star John Myatt, then a 19 year old first year student at Strathclyde, who was having a 'blinder' (and eventually finished 15th after only being 10th in the Scottish Universities). Afterwards we had a crazy night out in London. I just remember Dave and me cowering in the crammed back seat of a Mini as we drove from pub to pub. The undemonstrative Jim Wight, who was not normally known for joining us for a pint after races, sat in a corner with a smile on his face knocking back whisky after whisky without any apparent effect...'*

Ian Young's memory of the race itself is hazy after all these years: *'I don't recall [very much] about our stunning win in the BUSF Champs when I was first Scot and first EUHH home in eighth place. I do recall that I felt elated at that, but it was a long way off being first, second or third. I remember revelling in the mud and on the hills because, being light, I could skip over the glaur and Eddie Sinclair had me trained to use hills as an opportunity to 'break' the opposition, helped in no small way by the Arthur Lydiard-style training which Gareth [Bryan-Jones] and I used to put in on the ploughed fields around Loanhead.'*

Alex Wight has clearer recall about the course: *'BUSF '67 I had a good run but lost places on every lap in the muddy stretch at the end of the lap. I was also spiked on the first lap when someone landed on my left foot. The spike went straight in (through?). I felt no pain at the time, but remembered the incident when I found the hole in my foot afterwards'*

Dave Logue was overtaken by Chris Elson in the final 400 metres, to come in seventh man for EUHH, and narrowly fail to count for the team. *'It was a mud heap on Parliament Hill Fields'* he recalls *'not my kind of course. Also remember a lot of pissed people in a Mini, or was that after Hyde Park? These trips were all a blur especially returns at midnight Sunday on the last flight out of Heathrow.'*

Comparisons show that the British Universities win was an even more significant achievement than victory in the Scottish National event and it has only been emulated once since by a Scottish University, although the EUHH team was second in 1968. In the 'Scottish', the team won three times in this era (and remain the only University team to win the Scottish National Senior Mens Championships), despite having to spread their resources between the Senior and Junior races. In addition, in the sixty seven years between 1950 and 2017 EUHH won the Scottish National

Junior title 15 times (including four times in the 1960s and five times in a row in the 1990s). St Andrews have been victors in this event twice, Glasgow University once and Strathclyde once, a reflection in part of the average ages of university competitors.

There was a school of thought that the British Universities win in 1967 was not any more meritorious an achievement than the victory of the 1950 team, despite the number of competing teams being considerably greater. Jim Wight, with his logical mind, pointed out at the time that the main protagonists were always Oxford, Cambridge and London Universities and that applied as much to 1950 as it did to 1967. However, this scenario has changed over the years with more 'provincial' teams winning, including Birmingham University's astonishing run of seven victories, thanks initially to the inspiring leadership of Andy Holden, between 1971 and 1978, and specialist sports institutions such as Loughborough University have dominated the event in more recent years.

The Hyde Park Relay just a week after the British Universities Championships resulted in yet another record breaking win for EUHH, this time in 85:24, 1 minute 45 seconds clear of Sheffield University in second place. Again, this was a triumph of teamwork by a team without 'stars', all six runners completing their stage runs with times within 20 seconds of each other, at an average of 14:14 per leg.

The main club season ended for EUHH with the unique achievement of victory in both the Scottish Senior and Scottish Junior Cross Country Championships on the same day, 25 February 1967. Running in EUHH's now traditional bare feet, I was second (by one second) to Eddie Knox in the Junior race, with Dave Logue fifth, and the Senior team was led home by Jim Wight in 10th place and Alex Wight in 13th, in another triumph of close packing and team work. The Senior team's winning points margin of 144 was a record for the event and has only been exceeded once in the 50 years since[42].

Although 1966-67 was the peak year for EUHH in terms of the team's achievements, 1967-68, with Gareth Bryan-Jones now as captain, was arguably an even more successful season with a significant improvement in individual performances. Victory was achieved in the Edinburgh to Glasgow for the third time in a row although the winning time (which

---

[42] Cambuslang Harriers won the Senior title in 1992 by 148 points, from Racing Club, Edinburgh.

was always at the mercy of the wind direction, the prevailing south west wind heading down the A8 towards Edinburgh) was considerably slower than in the two previous years at 3:44:50, only 50 seconds ahead of Shettleston Harriers and Edinburgh Southern Harriers, who tied for second place. On this occasion, only Jim Wight (for the third successive year) was fastest individual on his leg. EUHH were the only university team ever to win the Edinburgh to Glasgow and, between its inception in 1930 and the final official race in 2002[43], they won five medals (including three gold), all between the years of 1964 and 1969. Glasgow University, who were bronze medal winners in 1960 and 1962, are the only other university team to have finished in the first three.

Gareth Bryan-Jones, fresh from his record breaking run in the British Universities steeplechase that summer, and I finished first and second respectively for Scotland against the English Northern Counties in Edinburgh in November 1967, first and second in the Nigel Barge Road Race and first and third (with Bill Ewing second) in the East Districts in January, with EUHH regaining the team title. We were both selected, along with Fergus Murray, now with Edinburgh Southern Harriers, to compete for Scotland in the San Sebastian International Cross Country event later in January, although all three of us performed below par on the muddy course at the Lasarte Hippodrome.

At that time cross country was administered world-wide by the International Cross Country Union and Scotland, as a founding member of the union, was invited to the ICCU championships as a separate nation each year, as were England, Wales and Northern Ireland. As a result, the Scottish Cross Country Union could select their own athletes to take part in the various invitation races held in Europe over the winter, most notably in France (for example, in Chartres), Spain (Granollers, Elgoibar and Bilbao, as well as San Sebastian) and Belgium (Hannut and the 'Martini' in Brussels). In 1973 the administration of cross country passed to the International Amateur Athletics Federation (now, in the 'open era', the International Association of Athletics Federations) who tolerated the separate 'home nations' until 1988, when they were combined into a British team, in line with athletics generally.

In 1968, the San Sebastian race coincided with the Scottish Universities Championships at Westerlands in Glasgow but, undeterred by the

---

[43] The event finally had to be shelved after 2002 due to increasing concerns about traffic and road safety, although attempts were made to hold unofficial versions of the event on minor roads for a few years after that.

absence of Gareth and me, the other EUHH runners performed to script, Dave Logue winning the race from Jim Wight with Alex Wight in fifth, Iain Hathorn sixth and Ian Young seventh as the team swept the board in the team race. 19 year old first year architecture student Andy McKean, later to become one of the finest cross country runners ever produced north of the border, was among the counting runners in eighth place.

With the exception of the Scottish Junior race, the only minor hiccup for the season was the team's narrow failure to retain the British Universities Championship title at Parliament Hill Fields. Behind the individual winner, English International Frank Briscoe of Leeds University, the second-placed EUHH team were spread between me in seventh place and Ian Young in 26th, giving a points total of 99, only 12 less than the winning team of the year before. Unfortunately for the team's prospects Gareth Bryan-Jones was taken ill that day and could only finish in 24th place after his outstanding performances earlier in the season. However, EUHH were 33 points adrift of Cambridge and would not have won in any event.

However, the Hyde Park Relay on 17 February saw the third successive win for the EUHH team and yet another record breaking performance, this time in 84:28, at an average of 14:05 per leg, with three runners, Jim Wight (13:58 on the first leg), Bryan-Jones (13:43) and me (13:48) joining the exclusive club of sub-14 minute performers for the first time.

Team victory followed in the Scottish Senior Championships, where, after leading for much of the race, albeit with spikes in *lieu* of bare feet on this occasion, I was narrowly beaten into second place, again by one second, by the fast finishing Lachie Stewart. Gareth Bryan-Jones was 10th, Dave Logue 13th, Iain Hathorn 19th, Alex Wight 24th and Jim Wight 25th, giving EUHH a one point victory over Aberdeen Athletic Club, who packed their six counting runners between ninth and 20th. Andy McKean led the third placed EUHH team home as seventh individual in the Junior event.

In common with all university sports teams, EUHH were at the mercy of the lengths of degree courses and personnel were constantly changing. In fact, several of the EUHH team in the 1960s, including Fergus Murray, Ian Young and Jim Wight, were able to take advantage of the success of the team by continuing their studies through postgraduate courses. Alex Wight, Chris Elson, Gareth Bryan-Jones (after a first degree at Leeds University), and later Jim Dingwall, were all PhD students, and others such as Andy McKean and me, who studied architecture, had the advantage, at least in our sporting endeavours, of being on longer than average first degree courses. Gareth Bryan Jones, Jim Wight, Chris Elson, Iain Hathorn and Alex Wight (who stayed on as a member of staff in the Computer Department) all completed their Edinburgh studies in 1968.

With such a major loss of key runners at the same time, the standard of the EUHH team performances fell away and, in November 1968, the team could only finish seventh in the Edinburgh to Glasgow. In fact, the only team success in 1968-69 was in the Scottish Universities, which was won for the fourth year in a row, with Andy McKean, who was to bridge the period between the great teams of 1965-66 and 1966-67, and younger runners such as Jim Dingwall, third in the individual race. The EUHH second team also took first place in their race, with the dogged Dave Taylor second in the individual. Given the changes in the team, the fifth place in the Hyde Park Relay in February 1969 was a highly creditable performance.

After 1968, although the team was no longer at the forefront in Scotland (with the exception of a determined third place in the Edinburgh to Glasgow in 1969) there were many pleasing individual performances including Dave Logue's second Scottish Universities title in 1970, prior to his move to study for a PhD at Glasgow University where he continued to perform at the highest level. I won the Eastern Districts individual title in 1970, and finished fourth in the British Universities and second in the Scottish Senior to Jim Alder in 1971. Andy McKean finished fourth in the Scottish Senior in 1972, and had runaway victories in an EUHH vest at the East Districts, the 'Scottish' and the British Universities in 1973, as a prelude to his wonderful achievements when a member of Edinburgh Athletic Club later in the 1970s.

Despite all the accolades about the team effort there could still be a fierce underlying rivalry between team members which accounted as much for the success of the club as team spirit. This was mainly because many of the principal opponents of the leading EUHH runners at the time were facing them across the EUHH changing room. Just as Ian Young, after his Scottish Universities win, would have been determined to be the first counter home for EUHH in the British Universities in 1967 so, equally, I no doubt would have wanted to make up for an otherwise indifferent winter season by outrunning the times of the other team members on my leg of the Hyde Park Relay that year. In a similar way, Gareth Bryan-Jones with his quiet, understated determination had set his sights on an Olympic place in 1968 and, with meticulous planning and extreme dedication, had achieved his goal. This applied to the more 'driven' ones but perhaps not to others who, with different and perhaps less obsessive priorities, saw the sport much more in recreational terms and were perhaps more likely to linger in, and enjoy the camaraderie of, the second team.

Many of those who stayed on to live in Edinburgh after graduation either ran for Edinburgh Southern Harriers or Edinburgh Athletic Club. Later on the legendary extrovert EUHH man, marathon runner and committee stalwart Robin Thomas, the inspiration behind the 'Triple Hundred'[44], was the driving force in the formation of a new club in the 1980s, Hunter's Bog Trotters[45], which was largely, at least in its early days, made up of former members of EUHH. The 'Trotters' went on to finish a narrow second to Mizuno Racing Club in the Edinburgh to Glasgow in 2001, after having established a significant lead at the final changeover, and won the Senior Mens National team race in 2001 and 2007, and the Womens in 2010 and 2016. On the individual front there have been many fine performances by Phil Mowbray (a former EUHH man and 13:49.44 5,000 metre runner on the track), Donald Naylor, Anne Buckley, Rosie Smith and others.

EUHH itself continues to thrive as a key section of the Edinburgh University Sports Union and a leading club at Scottish national level. Bolstered by the long overdue formation of a women's section in the mid 1970s, with Scottish International Violet Hope as the first Women's Captain, club membership is as healthy as ever, and the women's team in particular has enjoyed national and British Universities success in more recent years as a team and, at individual level, through the running of the likes of Gillian Palmer and Rhona Auckland.

But that is a story for others to recount.

---

[44] The 'Triple Hundred' involved running one hundred miles and drinking one hundred pints of beer, in the space of one hundred hours. The Guinness Book of Records allegedly refused to recognise this achievement as it was considered too negative an image for younger readers.

[45] Hunter's Bog, which takes its name from the royal hunting parties of the past, is the broad valley located between Arthur's Seat and Salisbury Crags in Holyrood Park in Edinburgh where runners often train, although Thomas, no doubt with a twinkle in his eye, introduced an element of irony into his choice of this less than salubrious title.

Chris Elson winning the East District mile title as a first year student at Meadowbank in May 1962. Hunter Watson (Edinburgh Athletic Club) finished second. Watson was a leading EUHH runner in the 1950s and subsequently a distinguished coach and veteran athlete.

XIII

Fergus Murray leads the mile field at Edinburgh University Sports at Craiglockhart in May 1965, from Alex Wight (31), Chris Elson and Ian Young (28).
(from collection of Fergus Murray, photographer unknown)

Gareth Evans negotiates
mud and glaur for the glory of EUHH in
the 1960s.
(from collection of Iain Hathorn,
photographer unknown)

The EUHH team following another successful team race in 1964 - 65 (l to r) Gareth Evans,
Fergus Murray, Frank Gamwell, Chris Elson, Roger Young, Ian Young, Alistair Matson, Jim
Wight.
(from collection of Fergus Murray, photographer unknown)

Alistair Blamire leads for EUHH from Ian Binnie (Victoria Park AAC) at the end of the first leg of the Edinburgh to Glasgow Relay, November 1965. Binnie jokingly accused Blamire of stealing a march by going round the roundabout at the Maybury in the wrong direction. This was the first of three successive wins in the event by EUHH.
(Brian Covell)

The EUHH team which won the Edinburgh to Glasgow Relay in November 1965:
(back row, l to r) Roger Young, Chris Elson, Willie Allan, Frank Gamwell, Iain Hathorn (Hon Sec)
(front row, l to r) Fergus Murray, Jim Wight, Alex Wight, Alistair Blamire.
(with kind permission of The Scotsman Publications Ltd/photographer unknown)

Gareth Bryan-Jones takes the water jump on the way to winning the 3,000 metres steeplechase at the British Universities Championships in May 1966. His winning time of 9 minutes 2.6 seconds was an improvement of over 20 seconds on his personal best time.
(from collection of Gareth Bryan-Jones, photographer unknown)

Victory 'Jigsaw' of the AAA 3,000 metres steeplechase final in July 1966. The athletes include Bill Ewing (5), Maurice Herriott (1), the eventual winner, Ernie Pomfret (13), Lachie Stewart (16) and Gareth Bryan-Jones (3). Bryan-Jones won the event in 1968 and gained selection for the Olympic Games in Mexico City.
(Photographer unknown)

10

EQUIPMENT

Shoes - cross country. These are designed for gripping in mud and snow. They are in stud or ripple form and cost around £3.

Road - Road shoes are essential for training and racing as incorrect footwear, such as sand shoes, can lead to injury. The most popular racing show is the canvas "Tiger Cub" which can be used for both cross country and road. Runners are advised to buy hard wearing, protective leather shoes for training.

Track Suit. The track suit is not essential but is a useful acquisition. A rugby jersey and jeans will do the job. "Edinburgh University" track suits are available.

Vests, shorts and supporters

are essential and the costs are around 10/-, 12/- and 10/- respectively. According to the constitution, our colours are green vest and white shorts.

CLUB RACES

The internal University races are the Arthur's Seat race, the inter faculty race over 3 miles, the Christmas handicap and in March the club champs. A medal is awarded in the latter to the first novice as well as to the winner.

Most runners contribute to "Athletics Weekly". Our results appear regularly. The price is 1/6d. and the profits of 6d. per copy go into the club funds. From these funds we bought a

Extract from the EUHH handbook 1966-67. Note the emphasis given to 'supporters'.
(Alistair Blamire)

Dave Logue (EUHH) hands over to Ian Young in the lead at Armadale Cross, at the end of the fourth stage of the Edinburgh to Glasgow Relay, November 1966. This was the second of EUHH's three successive wins in the event.
(Graham Orr)

Iain Hathorn competing in the Scottish Cross Country Championships at Hamilton Racecourse in February 1967. Willie Allan can be seen in the background.
(from collection of Iain Hathorn, photographer unknown)

Gareth Bryan-Jones and Iain Hathorn head back to King's Buildings on the EUHH course during the club championships, 1967.
(from collection of Iain Hathorn, photographer unknown)

Curious passers-by look on as Alex Wight sprints past the Serpentine at the Hyde Park
Relay, February 1967.
(from collection of Alex Wight, photographer unknown)

The EUHH team after the Scottish Cross Country Championships at Hamilton Racecourse
in February 1967:
(back row, l to r) Ian Young, Alex Wight, Jim Wight, Iain Hathorn, Dave Logue, Gareth
Bryan-Jones, Brian Jamieson
(front row, l to r) John Meldrum, Alistair Blamire, Willie Allan, Ken Fyfe
(from collection of Alistair Blamire, photographer unknown)

The lead runners in the Scottish Cross Country Championships at Hamilton Racecourse, February 1968 (l to r) Alistair Blamire (EUHH), John Linaker (Pitreavie), Lachie Stewart (Vale of Leven), the eventual winner, and Jim Wright (Edinburgh AC). (Graham Orr)

Iain Hathorn (r) pips Jack Macfie on the line in the 880 yards on the grass track at Craiglockhart, Edinburgh University Sports, May 1968. (Brain Covell, from collection of Iain Hathorn)

Gareth Bryan-Jones leads the steeplechase for Britain against Poland at the White City in 1968. Number 4 is John Jackson.
(from collection of Gareth Bryan-Jones, photographer unknown)

Andy McKean competing for EUHH in the Hyde Park Relay, February 1970.
(from collection of Andy McKean, photographer unknown)

Jim Dingwall negotiating the seventh stage of the Edinburgh to Glasgow Relay for Falkirk Victoria Harriers in 1985. He ran in the event 18 times, and equalled Andy McKean's stage record of 31:00 for the sixth leg in 1977.
(Graham MacIndoe)

Robin 'YP' Thomas competing for Hunters Bog Trotters in his veteran years.
(From collection of Robin Thomas, photographer unknown).

Chapter 4

PROFILES OF KEY EUHH INDIVIDUALS OF THE 1960s

The Forerunners of the British Universities Winning Team

MARTIN CRAVEN

Martin Craven was the most successful EUHH athlete between the departure of Adrian Jackson in 1960 and the emergence of Fergus Murray as an international runner, but he had left Edinburgh before the team really started to take off. Born in Hoylake and raised in Cheshire, Martin moved with his family to Burneside near Kendal in the 1950s and he joined Kendal Athletic Club as a youngster. He arrived in Edinburgh University in 1959 to study for an MA in History and Geography.

Martin's early performances for EUHH showed little promise of the success he was to achieve later on. He was a lowly 18th fastest on the third leg of the Edinburgh to Glasgow Relay in 1959, with the team well down the field in 17th place, although he had improved considerably by the following year, running the seventh fastest fifth leg as the team finished 10th. He was 37th in the Scottish Junior Cross Country Championships in his first year and improved to 20th in season 1960-61, with the team in third place, and 21st in 1961-62. No doubt influenced by the new approach to training which was developing at Edinburgh, his breakthrough year was 1962-63 when he improved significantly, finishing fifth in the Senior National at his first attempt, and being selected to run for Scotland in the International Cross Country Championships in San Sebastian. He was runner up in the Scottish Universities Championships that year (with EUHH victorious in the team race) as Calum Laing of Glasgow won the third of his three successive victories in the event, and was second of the Scottish universities contingent behind Mel Edwards of Aberdeen (although Alasdair Heron, running for Cambridge, was also ahead of him), in 13th place, in the Universities Athletic Union/British Universities Cross Country Championships (with the EUHH team seventh).

On the track, Martin was one of the few Scottish based runners to run under 14 minutes for three miles around this time, clocking 13:56.6 in third place (behind Ron Hill and Fergus Murray) in the British Universities Championships in 1963, after going through two miles in 9:12. The time ranked him third in Scotland for the year and he was ranked fifth in the six miles after finishing fourth in the Scottish Championships at Westerlands in 29:47.4, behind the stellar trio of Brown, Linaker and Wood. His career best time for three miles was 13:39.4, set in 1966, but his 10,000 metre best of 29:55.4 was achieved considerably later, in 1973, at the age of 32. He also ran 49:19.6 for ten miles when finishing third in the Scottish Championships over that distance in 1973.

However, it was on the roads, and particularly over longer distances, that he was most successful. After a couple of years of limited competition he recorded a time of 2:24:26 in his first attempt at the marathon, in winning the Preston to Morecambe race in 1966. The following year, after retaining this title in 2:20:58, he finished fifth in the AAA marathon and as a result was selected, along with Donald Macgregor, to compete for Britain in the classic Košice Peace Marathon in Czechoslovakia (now Slovakia) where he finished fourth in 2:23:14, only five weeks after the AAA race. Martin's best time of 2:18:38 was achieved in the AAA event in 1975 and, six years later, he ran 2:31:55 as a vet in the London Marathon.

He was a stalwart of the Edinburgh Southern Harriers team from the early 1970s onwards, competing for them in the Edinburgh to Glasgow on eleven occasions (which included five team wins), the last of which was in 1980 when, at the age of 39, he was second fastest on the seventh leg with the team finishing fourth. Martin, who continued to compete into his 60s, was renowned for wearing the ubiquitous Tiger 'Cubs', for training as well as racing, without any apparent consequences in terms of injury, and he earned the nickname 'The Crab' for his slightly eccentric running style.

Martin graduated from Edinburgh in 1963 and, after completing his Dip Ed at Oxford in 1965, he taught for four years in schools in England before returning to Edinburgh in 1970 to take up a post as a Careers Officer with City of Edinburgh Council where he stayed until his retirement. He would recall self-deprecatingly that he had advised a football-mad youngster that the odds were heavily stacked against a successful career in the sport and that he should consider a 'proper job'. The youngster was Gordon Strachan.

Martin Craven, a gentle, sociable man, died in 2013.

GARETH EVANS

Gareth Evans studied for an Arts degree at Edinburgh University between 1962 and 1966. He was a member of the EUHH team when it was beginning to free itself of the shackles of the *laissez faire* attitude to training which had become prevalent in the early 1960s after Adrian Jackson had graduated, even though Gareth, a naturally talented athlete, was not himself particularly renowned for training hard. At cross country he was a regular member of the first team and was second counter for EUHH at the 'Scottish' in 1965 when Fergus Murray won and the team finished third, and fifth counter for the team which finished fifth in the BUSF in the same year. Gareth was a highly convivial character, different from the introverted types who tended to drift into running from time to time.

On the track he was the first string for Edinburgh University at 880 yards from 1963 and finished second in this event at the Scottish Universities in 1965 on the grass track at Aberdeen in a time of 1:54.5. He ran a mile in 4:12.8 at Pitreavie in June that year, in finishing third in the annual East versus West match.

He left Edinburgh to study for a Dip Ed at Oxford University in 1966 and Fergus Murray, who was on the same course, recalls Gareth, the epitome of whatever 'cool' meant in those days, attending one of the lectures, leaning against a radiator in his dressing gown, eating an apple.

FRANK GAMWELL

Frank was from Dunfermline and was the archetypical mileage man and the rather unfair subject of an apocryphal tale that he dropped out of the Hyde Park Relay after two miles because he had completed his 100 miles for the week. More outgoing than most, Frank was a regular in the EUHH for much of his time at Edinburgh and, thanks to his committed and influential approach to training, was among the backbone of runners which saw EUHH metamorphose into the top team in Scotland by the mid 1960s. He was awarded his 'Blue' in 1964-65 and 1965-66. He ran in the Edinburgh to Glasgow four times, from 1962 to 1965, taking the record breaking Edinburgh team into the lead after running the fastest time on the fifth leg in his final year.

Frank was also a member of the winning EUHH teams at the Scottish Junior Cross Country Championships in 1964 (finishing 13th) and 1965 (14th), and the Senior team race in 1966 (18th). At the Hyde Park Relay he was in the EUHH team which won the event for the first time, setting a new course record, in 1966. He was timed at 14:22 for his leg. A committed team player, he was also in the winning EUHH teams at the Scottish Universities in 1965 (finishing sixth) and 1966 (eighth), and the East Districts in 1966 (11th).

After graduation he followed in the footsteps of Fergus Murray and joined Ilford Athletic Club in the summer of 1966. He stayed on to live in Ilford, meeting his future wife Sue there and, with John Batchelor (a British road running international who later studied for a PhD at Edinburgh University) and Roy Gill among his teammates, he became one of the Essex club's top runners for several years, winning the county 20 Miles Road Race Championship in 1967 in 1:47:25. However, he maintained contact with his former EUHH team mates and was a great supporter at the British Universities in London in February 1967.

His best track times were all achieved in 1967 when running for Ilford including 9:13.4 for two miles (at Hornchurch on 2 May 1967), 14:17.8 for three miles (at Cricklefield on 2 September 1967), 29:33.0 for six miles (at Cricklefield on 13 August 1967) and 9:35.4 for the 3,000 metres steeplechase (at Withdean on 22 July 1967). He ran 2:40:52 for the marathon in the Polytechnic event in 1966, although his 20 mile time suggests that he had the potential to run this distance considerably faster.

Frank's degree was in Forestry and, after working in the timber industry in the south east of England, he returned to Scotland in the mid 1970s to set up a private forestry business near Auchterarder which he ran until his death at the age of 70 in 2014.

ROGER YOUNG

Roger Young discovered early on at primary school that he was good at running. He found this gratifying and, without taking the sport particularly seriously, he went on to compete for his school team at Gordonstoun in 1961, finishing third in the North of Scotland Schools Championships, which were regularly held at the school. He arrived at Edinburgh in 1962 as an 18 year old on a Rolls Royce Scholarship to study Mechanical Engineering. With the added pressure of the endowment, he took his course work very seriously but found time for training and made the first team in his freshman year, making the first of four successive appearances in the Edinburgh to Glasgow Relay.

Inspired by Jim Peters and Ron Clarke, he found the training methods at

Edinburgh far ahead of many of the other clubs in Scotland, and managed up to 70 miles a week in the company of Elson and Murray, when studies allowed. Another role model was the Olympic marathon champion, Abebe Bikila of Ethiopia, who first won the title in 1960, padding his way barefoot to victory down the Appian Way in Rome chased home by his great rival Rhadi Ben Abdesselam of Morocco. Roger later emulated Bikila by training occasionally in bare feet on the roads near his 'digs' in Newington and found it 'fine, until you hit gravel'. He often ran barefoot on the track as many of the races then were on grass[46].

Roger considers his best performance finishing second, running in bare feet, to Ian McCafferty in the Scottish National Junior race in 1965, which led to his selection for the Scottish Senior Team for the International Championships in Ostend that year. Unfortunately, he had to withdraw from the team as the trip coincided with exams and his tutor, who was actually a 'stand in' for his Professor (who had died suddenly), would not permit him time off. This was symptomatic of the attitudes of the time – a sense of disapproval came from all fronts whether from anxious parents, from negative tutors and employers, or from a 1960s society that was increasingly suspicious of competition as a healthy approach to advancement.

Roger, who was captain of EUHH in 1964-65, improved as an athlete year on year and was consistently at or near the front in East District and Scottish National cross country events during his time at Edinburgh. He finished second in the East Districts in 1965, with EUHH winning the team race, and was a highly respectable 11th in the British Universities Championships at Nottingham that year, as the team finished fifth.

He considers his third place behind Jim Alder in the Brampton to Carlisle ten mile road race in November 1964, in a time of 50:14, as one of his more satisfying achievements. However, course work continued to take precedence and training tailed off in his final year, although he was second counter for EUHH in the East Districts, the Scottish Universities and the Scottish Senior Cross Country Championships (finishing eighth in his only attempt at this race) with the team winning on each of these occasions.

---

[46] Barefoot running was originally popularised in Britain by Bruce Tulloh who won the 5,000 metres at the European Championships, sprinting to victory in bare feet on the cinder track in Belgrade in 1962. Ron Hill, Tim Johnston and Jim Hogan were also renowned for running in bare feet on cinders and Hogan regularly ran barefoot in cross country events, dismissing the risks involved on courses which were often open to the public.

His best track times of 14:20.6 for three miles, set in early May 1964 at the age of 20, and 30:00.8 for six miles and 9:47.2 for the 3,000 metres steeplechase, both set in 1965, do not reflect his talent or potential. Most of his track running was done in April and May each year, more often than not on the grass track at Craiglockhart. He undoubtedly could have run a lot faster later on in the year, and indeed if he had continued running seriously into his mid to late twenties, but he didn't appear to compete beyond the University season each year. However, he did manage to appear in the British Universities track championships on one occasion, at Iffley Road, Oxford in 1964, where he ran the three miles.

One of his favourite anecdotes from his running days relates to the Edinburgh to Glasgow Relay in November 1965. It was the first time EUHH won the event and the favourable following wind helped the team to a new record. Roger ran the last leg and, as the lead runner, was expecting to be handed the ceremonial baton a couple of hundred yards from the finish, containing a message from the Edinburgh Lord Provost to his Glasgow counterpart. But there was no baton and no Lord Provost and the only official at the finish was the timekeeper - everyone else, including the baton and its intended recipient, was in a nearby watering hole. So, after completing the race, Roger was told to run back up the course and do the finish again once the Lord Provost had emerged from the pub.

After graduating in 1966, due to pressure of work and a need to satisfy his lifelong passion for recreational flying, he never ran competitively again, and only kept running for fitness, eventually giving up altogether in his 40s following operations, which were only partially successful, on both his knees.

Roger Young was latterly Chief Executive of Scottish Hydro-Electric, retiring in 1999, and now lives in Comrie in Perth and Kinross.

* * *

The British Universities Winning Team

IAN YOUNG

Springburn Harriers in Glasgow was a breeding ground of young distance running talent in the early 1960s, under the tutelage of Eddie Sinclair, who had represented Scotland in the International Cross Country Championships in 1960. Ian Young found that he could outrun most of his contemporaries at school and, inspired by the achievements of world stars like Herb Elliott, he joined the Springburn club at the age of 15. There, he met and began training with the likes of Eddie Knox, later to have considerable success at UK junior level including victory in the International Junior Cross Country Championships in 1967, and Duncan Middleton, a very talented half miler who set a Scottish record and represented Britain at that event in the same year.

With the help of Sinclair's methods, and the support of his parents, Ian began training systematically and finished second (to Ian McCafferty) in the Scottish National Youths Cross Country Championships in 1963. He went on to become the first winner of the Scottish Schools Cross Country Championships and winner of the mile, in 4:27.0, at the Scottish Schools track championships at Goldenacre in the same year. He also represented Scotland in the British Schools International at Meadowbank in Edinburgh in 1963, and the Scottish Junior team in the International Cross Country Union Championships in Dublin in 1964, where he was a team mate of McCafferty, finishing 22nd. It was in Dublin that he first met his hero Fergus Murray, who had just won the first of his three Scottish National senior titles.

Ian's decision to study at Edinburgh, where he graduated with an MA and BCom, was based almost entirely on his desire to develop his distance running career through training with Fergus Murray and company. He went straight into the EUHH first team in season 1964-65 and, after finishing sixth in the Scottish National Junior Cross Country Championships, gained a second junior vest in the International Championships in Ostend, finishing 17th. By regularly training up to 100 miles a week, often in the company of Gareth Bryan-Jones, and occasionally with me, Ian was the leading EUHH runner in season 1966-67, when the club was at its most successful as a team. He ran the second fastest time (by one second) on the fifth leg of the Edinburgh to Glasgow Road Relay, and he led the winning EUHH team home in eighth place in the British Universities Cross Country Championships in London. He was also Scottish Universities cross country and three mile champion in 1967 and represented Scotland in various cross country events throughout his Edinburgh career. He ran the three miles in 14:01.6 in finishing second behind Gareth Bryan-Jones at the East District Championships at Meadowbank in May 1967.

Ian was an extremely focussed athlete, particularly in 1966-67, and it was a great disappointment to him when he ran indifferently at the Scottish Championships in February 1967, finishing 15th of the Scottish runners (the visiting New Zealand team were running as guests) and failing to make the Scottish Senior team for the International Championships in Wales, particularly since his form over the season would have virtually guaranteed selection. However, he gained a great sense of personal achievement from his success in athletics. Unfortunately he suffered latterly from Achilles tendon problems and was greatly missed when he was forced to retire from the sport at the relatively young age of 25 in 1970.

Ian Young, with his friendly banter and droll bonhomie, looks back fondly on his time at Edinburgh as one of the most enjoyable periods of his life, as he mixed his studies and sport with other outside interests. He was an entrepreneur even as a student, running a music club in his home town of Kirkintilloch, 'The Graveyard', which attracted well-known bands from the Glasgow area, and later the 'Bird Cage' boutique in the centre of the town. He took over his father's brass foundry business in Kirkintilloch after graduating from University and developed the business into one of the leading foundry and engineering companies in Britain, specialising in every metal except steel, and trading in many countries world-wide. He was awarded an OBE in 2006 for services to engineering in Scotland, primarily for 25 years of involvement in foundry training and setting national standards in the engineering industry.

JIM WIGHT

The quietly determined Jim Wight followed his brother Alex to Edinburgh University from Duns in 1962 to study mathematics. Born in October 1944 he was in the junior age group at cross country right through to the final year of his first degree, when he finished sixth at the Scottish National Junior Cross Country Championships in 1966 as the team finished third after three successive wins. He became a regular in the EUHH first team by the time of his second year as a student and was a key member of the winning teams in the Edinburgh to Glasgow Relay in 1965, 1966, and 1967, running the fastest individual time for the seventh stage on each occasion and setting a stage record in 1965. After having remained in Edinburgh to study for a Diploma in Education at Moray House College, Jim was in the Hyde Park winning teams in 1967 and 1968 (when he ran his leg in 13:58), the British Universities team in 1967 (when he was second counter in the winning team), and he performed with distinction in the Scottish Universities, including second place to Dave Logue in 1968.

Jim's optimum training mileage of 60-70 miles a week, while ideal for his light frame, was perhaps too low for him to exploit fully his great natural talent at longer distances including the marathon and ultra events. However, he continued to improve as he got older and, after leaving university in 1968, and as a member of Edinburgh Athletic Club, he had many successes on the roads including victory in the Edinburgh to North Berwick 22 mile race in 1969 in 2:00:54. He won the Morpeth to Newcastle in 1972 from Jim Alder, after dramatically pulling away from the Morpeth man on the road into Gosforth, and also finished third in this event in 1970, and fourth in 1973.

Jim ran for Scotland in the International Cross Country Championships in Cambridge in 1972 after his best ever placing of sixth in the Scottish Championships that year, and was selected for Scottish teams for several cross country races on the continent in the 1970s. Perhaps his best performance in this area of the sport was his 17th place in the English Championships at Sutton Coldfield in 1972.

He represented Scotland in the 1974 Commonwealth Marathon in Christchurch after finishing only 34 seconds behind Donald Macgregor, in 2:18:24, in the Scottish trials in 1973. In both 1969 and 1972 he finished second in the Two Bridges 36 mile road race (the latter behind brother Alex's record winning time), before eventually emulating Alex's achievement by winning the event in 1974. Among his other outstanding performances were victories in the Highgate Marathon in 1969 in 2:24:28, and the Harlow Marathon in 1974 in 2:16:28. His best ever marathon time of 2:15:43, behind Alex in the Edinburgh to North Berwick race in 1971, ranked him sixth in Britain for that year. On the track, he ran 14:17.0 for 5,000 metres in 1972 and 29:22.0 for 10,000 metres in 1973.

Jim Wight latterly worked for the Newcastle University Computing Laboratory, the service arm of the Computing Department of the University, and stayed on to live in the Newcastle area after his retirement.

GARETH BRYAN-JONES

Gareth Bryan-Jones, who was from Cheshire, of Welsh parentage, was 'hooked' at the age of eleven by seeing Gordon Pirie win the English National Cross Country Championships by a 'country mile' at Arrow Park, Birkenhead in 1954. Later on, he was inspired by the achievements of Peter Snell through reading Lydiard's classic book on coaching, *'Run to the Top'*. He was introduced to cross country at school when rugby (as usual) was cancelled due to the weather, and two teachers started a running team when Gareth was in fifth year. He represented Cheshire in the English Schools Championships in his final year at school.

At Leeds University, where Gareth studied Bacteriology, he mixed running with climbing at first and appeared for the second and third teams at cross country. However a serious accident to one of his hands resulted in him having to forgo climbing and he began to concentrate more seriously on running. The captain of the cross country team at Leeds at the time was a Yorkshireman, Dennis Quinlan, who had an Irish connection and competed for Ireland in the International Cross Country Championships in 1968 in Tunisia (where he was first counter for the Irish team) and in 1969 at Clydebank.

Quinlan was a stickler for organised training (and later a distinguished coach) and he had the members of the first team, which included Gareth by his final year, keep training diaries on which he would comment on a regular basis, with a target of 50 miles a week. The Leeds team was especially successful in 1964-65, finishing third in the British Universities (with Gareth in the counting six, in 42nd place, in the individual race) and winning the Hyde Park Relay with Gareth running 14:31 for his stage. In his final track season at Leeds in 1965, Gareth gave a glimpse of things to come by finishing second in the 3,000 metres Steeplechase at the Universities Athletic Union Championships and he represented the UAU in the match against the RAF and the Southern Counties.

Attracted in part by what he had heard about the student running scene in Scotland, he came up to Edinburgh in 1965 to study for a PhD in Microbiology. He settled in quickly to the Edinburgh regime of hard training and equally hard socialising, and soon became a pivotal member of the cross country team and eventually, along with Fergus Murray, Edinburgh University's most successful track athlete. Chris Elson was in the related discipline of Bacteriology and came over to introduce himself in the lab at King's Buildings, while Dave Logue (who started at Edinburgh in the same year) and Fergus became regular training companions and ultimately lifelong friends. All the talk among the EUHH runners in Gareth's first term was of the Edinburgh to Glasgow Relay but unfortunately he was injured negotiating a barrier in the East District Relays and failed to make the 'blue riband' event that year.

However, Gareth improved steadily throughout 1965-66, finishing fourth in the Scottish Universities (with the team first), 35th in the British Universities (team fifth), and 17th in the Scottish Senior Championships (team first). In the Hyde Park he was second fastest individual for the record breaking EUHH team, and eleventh fastest overall, with a time of 14:10. However, it was on the track, his main forte, where he surprised the sceptical Edinburgh University Athletic Club committee by winning the British Universities 3,000 metres Steeplechase from the front at Loughborough in May 1966 in 9:02.6, with Bill Ewing of Aberdeen, later to become the Scottish Champion and Native Record Holder at the event, second in 9:07.0. This win in 1966, which was an improvement of over twenty seconds on his personal best time, was not as much of a surprise to Gareth himself as it was to his teammates and rivals.

In the winter of 1965-66, unable to fit in the official EUHH training sessions on Wednesday afternoons, he had borrowed *'Run to the Top'* from Morningside Library and, by carefully following the schedules, often with Ian Young as a training companion, he had focussed on the British Universities track championships, in the Lydiard manner, as his target event for the year. This gave him the confidence to improve by such a huge margin in one race and he lowered his time further to 9 minutes dead at the AAA Championships in July that year. The Loughborough race was the first of three successive victories for Gareth at the British Universities, including a championship record win in 8:52.4 at Motspur Park in 1967. Unfortunately the assurances he received from the British Universities officials that he would be selected for the World Student Games in Tokyo in 1967 did not materialise. However, this slight gave him huge motivation to make a serious bid for Olympic selection in 1968, with the AAA Championships (and British Olympic trials) as his new target.

Although, during EUHH's successful 1966-67 cross country season, Gareth had continued to be a very important member of the team, it was in 1967-68 that he made a major breakthrough over the winter season, winning the Scotland versus English Northern Counties race in Edinburgh in November 1967[47] and the East Districts, from Bill Ewing, in January 1968, and finishing 10th in the Scottish Senior Championships in February of the same year as the team won by one point from Aberdeen AAC. Gareth also illustrated his potential as a major player over the summer by running 13:43 for the third fastest individual performance (behind England Internationalists Frank Briscoe and Mike Tagg) for his leg of the Hyde Park Relay as the team won in record breaking time for the third year in a row. He won the first of his three Scotland 'caps' in the International Cross Country Championships in 1968, finishing 47th in the

---

[47] This race was held on the road as cross country events were suspended during the 1967 foot and mouth epidemic.

senior race in Tunisia, and also represented Scotland in the San Sebastian Invitation Cross Country race in January of that year.

On the track, after competing for Wales in the three miles in the Home International on the new all-weather track at Grangemouth in 1967 Gareth, who remained in Edinburgh to do further research after completing his doctorate in June 1968, represented Scotland in the same match at the same venue the following year, winning the 3,000 metres Steeplechase after a fierce battle with the British record holder and Olympic silver medallist Maurice Herriott. Gareth had already achieved the Olympic qualifying standard (of 8:45.0) by pacing himself to a time of 8:40.6 in a Scottish League race six days earlier at Grangemouth and, aware from a discussion with Lachie Stewart that Herriott's races always tended to be dependent on a strong finish, he decided to push the pace from the gun. The two athletes were locked together throughout the race, with Gareth in the lead and Herriott on his shoulder (and Bill Ewing only a few seconds adrift, on the way to a Native Record), and they reached the bell in a very fast 7 minutes 28 seconds. However, by now they were both almost out on their feet and Gareth just managed to hold on by less than a second, winning in a then personal best of 8:38.2.

However, he still made space for races at club level in his final year at University, setting a new record of 13:44.2 for the three miles at the University Sports at Craiglockhart in May 1968. He recalls one occasion where he used an inter-varsity three mile race (which he won) as an interval running training session (12 x 220 yards with 220 jog between) incurring, in the same way as Fergus Murray a few years earlier, the wrath of some of the EUAC officials who perhaps did not identify with the level of dedication they were witnessing.

The result of the Grangemouth runs was Gareth's first British 'vest', teaming up with John Jackson against Switzerland in Zurich on 30 June, and finishing in second place. However, his target event for 1968 was the AAA Steeplechase Championships and British Olympic trials on 12 and 13 July. Here he produced perhaps his greatest career performance, pushing the pace in the final from the fifth lap and making his move with 300 metres to go to head off the challenges of Jackson and Herriott and achieve an emphatic victory in the second fastest ever time by a Briton at that time[48]. It was typical of Gareth's incredibly focussed approach to training and competition that, in his earlier race against Herriot, he had

---

[48] Herriott set the British record of 8:32.4 in finishing runner-up to Gaston Roelants in the Olympic final in Tokyo in 1964. Gareth's winning time at the 1968 AAAs was 8:36.2.

struggled to win narrowly but here, at the White City in July, when it really mattered, he peaked superbly to see off the opposition in style and secure his selection for the Mexico Games.

It is well documented that the rarefied atmosphere in Mexico City was a huge disadvantage for distance runners from low altitude countries[49] and this, of course, also affected Gareth. Before the steeplechase event he and John Jackson had tended to train together and, in preparation for the qualifying heats, they ran a 9:07 steeplechase (with an extra hurdle *in lieu* of the water jump) on the training track, running at the even pace which they calculated was their best hope of reaching the final.

However, these good intentions went out the window in Gareth's heat when the little known Kenyan, Amos Biwott, set off with overzealous enthusiasm at a fast but uneven pace, taking the rest of the field with him. Gareth was fifth at the bell, one place outside the qualifying positions for the final, but a combination of negative thinking, and the image of the distressing condition in which he had seen Herriott at the end of his heat, resulted in him dropping two places in the last lap to finish seventh. Jackson and Herriot were no more successful, finishing fifth and eighth respectively in their own heats. The surprising Biwott prevailed in the final two days later.

Back home in the autumn, by now on a two year post-doctorate programme at Edinburgh University, and running for Edinburgh Southern Harriers, Gareth was able to take advantage of his Olympic level training schedule by running the sixth leg of the Edinburgh to Glasgow relay in 31:46, the same time as Lachie Stewart and 15 seconds faster than Ian Stewart.

In the Athletics Weekly Questionnaire published on 1 February 1969, Gareth, by now an established internationalist and approaching his peak, described his training as follows:

Winter:

Sunday – 15-18 miles cross country run. **Monday** – a.m. 6 miles steady; p.m. 15 miles fairly hard steady. **Tuesday** – a.m. 6 miles

---

[49] This was always considered to be Ron Clarke's last chance to win an Olympic Gold Medal but he finished sixth in the 10,000 metres, collapsing from lack of oxygen and remaining unconscious for ten minutes at the end of the race. Despite this, he also competed in the 5,000 metres, with the heats only two days later, but he sustained permanent heart damage as a result and later in life had to have a heart valve replaced.

steady; p.m. 8-10 miles *fartlek*. **Wednesday** – 10 miles *fartlek*. **Thursday** - a.m. 6 miles steady; p.m. 10 miles *fartlek*. **Friday** – 6 miles jog. **Saturday** - Race

Total mileage for week – c. 90

Summer:

Sunday – 15-18 miles steady. **Monday** – midday 3 miles steady, 3 x 1,500m steeplechase, 3 miles steady; evening 5 miles *fartlek*. **Tuesday** – midday 9 miles *fartlek*; evening 3 miles of 50 yard dashes. **Wednesday** – midday 3 miles steady, 10 x steeplechase laps, 3 miles steady; evening interval 220s and 440s. **Thursday** - 11 miles *fartlek*. **Friday** – 6 miles jog. Saturday - Race

Total mileage for week – c. 80

He also had one stint of running 140 miles a week for ten weeks in a row.

Gareth combined his regular training with sessions which simulated the unique circumstances of the steeplechase, running intervals over hurdles on the track at Craiglockhart or breaking up his rhythm by sprinting and jogging between lamp posts on the road or on the grass at Peffermill playing fields. He was also known to utilise the relatively soft landing which long jumps pits offered, to help him refine his water jump technique.

Interestingly, in the AW Questionnaire Gareth, faced with the added pressure of being expected to win every time he ran in Scotland, commented that 'the danger in athletics is that when too much is at stake it ceases to be a sport. The enjoyment starts to diminish as the pressure comes on. Satisfaction then seems to be more from achievements than from the actual participation'. This calls into question the comments of runners, however distinguished, who say how much they 'enjoy' a particular race or event. They can't possibly enjoy the nerves beforehand and the sheer effort and discomfort of the race itself, but they can enjoy the afterglow of a good performance – what Donald Macgregor once referred to as 'post-race euphoria' [50].

In February 1969, Gareth finished ninth in the Scottish Cross Country Championships and had his best run in the International (hosted by

---

[50] In 'Who's Who in British Athletics', Athletics Weekly, 20 December 1969.

Scotland at Clydebank), finishing forty third. The Scottish team was fifth. Then, in July of that year, he was in such great form that he found it easier to run 8:41.6 for his heat at the AAA Championships when 8:59 would have sufficed to qualify for the final. The following day, in the final, Gareth was convinced he had the British record in his sights and was about to make his move when he fell at the water jump on the fifth lap, chipping a bone his ankle and damaging ligaments, and putting himself out of action for the rest of the season.

Although he had already decided for reasons of conscience not to make himself available for selection for the 1969 European Championships in Greece, then under the control of the military junta, this appeared at first to be a major blow as it was so close to the Commonwealth Games in Edinburgh the following year. However, he recovered relatively quickly and was able to walk using crutches, and by October 1969 was back to full training and competing in cross country events as well as the Edinburgh to Glasgow Relay which his new club, Edinburgh Southern, won. He was selected for the Scottish team for the International Cross Country Championships in March 1970 despite an indifferent run in the Scottish Championships in Ayr and ran well, ahead of Dick Taylor and just behind Jim Alder, in the Hannut invitation international race in Belgium that winter.

His international career on the track resumed against East Germany in June 1970 and by July he was back to his best finishing fourth (and first Briton) in the steeplechase at the Commonwealth Games in Edinburgh in his best ever time of 8:33.8, one place behind the Olympic Champion, Biwott. He also ran for Britain in the European Cup Final that year, finishing second behind the future European Champion, Jean-Paul Villain of France.

Gareth Bryan-Jones was Scottish Champion at the steeplechase on five occasions including the 1969 race when he misjudged the finishing line and, when a straightforward victory seemed assured, was almost caught on the tape by me, the two of us sharing the Crabbie Cup for the most meritorious performance of the championships. However, after a successful season in 1971, and although still at the forefront in Scotland and competing regularly for Edinburgh Southern in British League races, his form gradually tailed off and, after being badly injured in a road accident in 1972, he began to take a serious interest in orienteering.

His best time for 5,000m was 13:56.0 which he set at the inaugural meeting at the new Edinburgh University track at Peffermill in May

1969, but clearly he could have run a faster time at this event in more competitive circumstances. His other best times on the track included 3:51.6 for 1,500 metres and 29:44.0 for 10,000 metres while in the marathon he recorded a time of 2:23:47 in the North Berwick race in May 1971, behind the Wight brothers and Donald Macgregor.

Gareth eventually joined his local club in Stirling, Forth Valley AC, and enjoyed many years (and indeed, still does, in his mid-seventies) of competitive orienteering and fell running. He has assisted with the organisation of the Scottish Six Day Event which, in 2015, incorporated the World Orienteering Championships and he continues to be involved in similar events. He ran the 96 mile West Highland Way from Milngavie to Fort William in under 24 hours at the age of 62, and was the first person over 70 years of age to complete the race in 2013. His three children all take a healthy interest in running and his elder daughter Kirsty, a member of Dark Peak Fell Runners, has been particularly successful at fell running and is a British Orienteering internationalist.

Gareth worked for The Distillers Company (which later became part of Diageo) near Stirling, retiring in 2001. He still lives in Stirling with his wife Jan, who has been a great supporter, informal mentor and social convener for the old EUHH team.

ALISTAIR BLAMIRE

I fell for sport from an early age and started taking a detailed interest in athletics after reading in the newspapers about the Bannister versus Landy 'Mile of the Century' in Vancouver in 1954 (with Landy looking over his inside shoulder on the last bend) and then winning the handicap obstacle race at George Heriot's School in 1956 - the School Games were like the Olympics to wee boys back then. I also recall watching the 1958 AAA Championships, when Graham Everett of Shettleston Harriers defeated Murray Halberg in the mile, and the 1958 Empire Games in Cardiff, where Herb Elliott had a starring role, on television.

Childish enthusiasm resulted in me organising distance races as a primary age schoolboy, round the playground or the local park, where 'Kuts' and 'Pirie' would reprise their battles from the 1956 Olympics, often with a different outcome. Serious training began in fifth year at Dumfries Academy when, after buying Franz Stampfl's book *'Running'* in a local bookstore and, following the schedules, I managed to improve my mile time by twenty seconds with 5 weeks of interval running in the spring of 1963, running 4:30.1 on the grass track at the school playing fields at Marchmont in Dumfries. I was second in the Scottish Schools Under-17 mile that year. I found training incredibly liberating, especially at the beginning. By following a schedule on your own you could improve beyond recognition and setting new school records was almost routine, especially when you were fairly sure that none of your predecessors would have trained as systematically. It was a significant confidence booster but, although there was great rapport with athletes and sportspeople from other events at Dumfries Academy at the time, the training itself was a very solitary activity.

Over the winter of 1963-64 I met Lewis Howitt, a psychology graduate from Glasgow University and local runner, who also happened to train at Marchmont and, on Howitt's recommendation, joined his club, Shettleston Harriers, and began competing in cross country events, finishing ninth in the Scottish National Youths Cross Country Championships and second in the Scottish Schools Cross Country Championships in 1964. At that time I was still playing rugby for Dumfries Academy, despite the risk of injury which was never too much of an issue back then.

In the summer of 1964 I reduced my best times to 4:20.9 for the mile and 4:21.7 for the 1,500 metres steeplechase. I won the Scottish Schools steeplechase in record time that year and represented Scottish Schools and Scottish Juniors in the company of Roddy Campbell of Daniel Stewart's College, who finished second in the AAA Junior Steeplechase later in the year. By this time, enthused by a subscription to Athletics Weekly, I also joined the British Milers' Club and started to look beyond Scotland for competition, although the schedules in Stampfl's book were inexplicably lacking in the core distance work necessary to sustain performances over the whole season and to compete successfully at cross country. However, Lewis Howitt obliged by taking me for an alleged ten mile run over the country before I left school.

At Edinburgh University, awe-inspired by my celebrated teammate Fergus Murray, I began to take on the ideas of Chris Elson, increasing training to 40 miles a week and competing for the EUHH first team. I was fourth on the first leg of the Edinburgh to Glasgow Road Relay in 1964, when EUHH finished second to Motherwell YMCA Harriers, and recall running in shoes borrowed from Frank Gamwell as the yachting pumps I had been training in had resulted in shin soreness. This was an ailment which dogged my running career and meant that I had to train on grass a lot of the time, especially as training mileage increased. However, this probably gave me an advantage over the country and I recovered from injury to finish ninth in the Scottish National Junior Cross Country Championships in 1965. In the summer of 1965 I won the Scottish Junior mile title and, at the age of 18, improved to 4:14.6 at Uxbridge, running for Scottish Universities versus the RAF.

My track career stalled for several years but I managed to continue improving on the road and the country, finishing third in the Scottish National Junior Championships in 1966 and being selected to compete in the International Junior in Rabat, Morocco, where I finished 15th. I was captain of EUHH in 1966-67 finishing second (by just one second) to Eddie Knox in the Scottish National Junior in 1967 and was selected for the Scottish team in the International Senior Championships in Barry, Wales, the first of five appearances as a senior in the global event.

The summers of 1966 and 1967 were spent in the company of Frank Gamwell in Ilford and, although my times on the track did not improve much, I began training up to 70 miles a week in preparation for the Harlow Marathon in October 1967 where, running for Ilford AC, I finished eighth in 2:29:47. Although the time is mediocre by today's standards, this proved to be similar in many ways to the epiphany of Iain Hathorn at the Ben Nevis Race in 1966, or indeed Fergus Murray in the 1962-63 season. The increased training mileage for the marathon gave me the confidence to improve markedly in 1967-68, finishing second in the Scotland versus English Northern Counties race in November 1967, fourth in the Morpeth to Newcastle, third in the East Districts and second (yet again by one second) to Lachie Stewart in the Scottish Senior Cross Country Championships in 1968. During the summer of 1968 I improved my three mile time by 39 seconds, to 13:37.0, and ranked fourth in Scotland for the steeplechase in my one attempt at the event that summer.

Over the winter of 1968-69 I won the Scottish International Trial, held at Dreghorn on the edge of the Pentland Hills in Edinburgh, from a strangely lethargic Ian McCafferty in November but the season was derailed in January 1969 when I suffered from a collapsed lung (spontaneous pneumothorax) after an EUHH *fartlek* session, which put out me out of action for several weeks. However, undeterred by warnings of a recurrence, recovery was relatively quick and by April I ran 13:54.2 for the three miles against Alastair Wood on the grass track at Aberdeen.

A successful track season followed, including a championship record of 8:50.6 (which stood for 32 years) for the steeplechase in the British Universities in June, Scottish National (8:41.4, at the White City, London) and Native (8:46.2, at Grangemouth) records in this event, and three British 'caps' against Czechoslovakia, Italy and France. In 1969-70 I finished third in the 'Morpeth', second to Mike Tagg of England in an invitation cross country race in Bilbao in January and third (first Briton) in the International Students Cross Country Championships in Berne in February 1970. I won the East District Cross Country Championships for the only time, and ran a 13:42 leg for the fourth placed EUHH team in the Hyde Park Relay that winter.

In 1970, the year of the Commonwealth Games in Edinburgh, injury and illness (including a second pneumothorax) put paid to my prospects and I never fully recovered the level of the 1969 season. For various reasons inconsistency became a theme but I still managed to finished second in the Scottish National Senior Championships (by 6 seconds, to Jim Alder) in 1971, fourth in the British Universities that year, and 11th in the English National Cross Country Championships in Norwich where I joined up with Lachie Stewart, Dick Wedlock (who had rejoined from Motherwell YMCA), Norman Morrison, Henry Summerhill and Tom Grubb to take the team title with Shettleston Harriers, the last such success by a Scottish club.

After winning the Scottish steeplechase title in 1972, I was runner-up in the 'Morpeth' in January 1973, and led the Scottish rankings with 8:43.8 for the steeplechase that year. However, I was not selected for the 1974 Commonwealth Games, despite achieving the recommended standard set by the SAAA. I continued to run reasonably well in the Scottish National Cross Country Championships and also dabbled in fell running later on (setting a new record for the Carnethy Hill Race in 1975) but my performances tailed off in the late 1970s. In the classic Three Peaks race in the Pennines in 1976 I ran out of steam on the descent from Ingleborough, finishing fourth after leading on the final summit, the result of carbo depletion and a foolish and misguided attitude to fluid consumption during the race.

Seventy miles a week was my optimum training mileage with a mixture of long and medium distance runs, *fartleks* and interval running on grass. The session I most remember was the 12 x 300 metres with 100 metres jog between which Dave Logue, Albie Smith, Innes Mitchell and I battled through at Westerlands, Glasgow during 1973-74. We liked to think it was a 15 minute three miles run as an interval session. Even Gerschler might have been impressed, despite the fact that we eschewed the cinder track for the grass rugby pitches nearby.

There are many anecdotes from my time in athletics. Along with Iain Hathorn, who was EUHH secretary at the time, I helped to organise the original EUHH Annual Dinner which was held at the University Gym of all places, in 1967, thanks to the support of Captain Stan Garner, who was the athletics manager on the Edinburgh University staff for many years. The dinner became a regular event in the EUHH calendar, later switching to the Minto Hotel in Newington. I also recall training from my grandmother's house in Gilmore Place, Edinburgh with Fergus Murray in freezing fog, the two of us returning an hour later, looking forty years older, with each individual hair on our heads coated in ice. A killer ten mile fartlek on the Braid Hills was another training 'highlight' with Fergus later on, especially as it was accomplished immediately after a heavy dinner of stew of questionable provenance, and tinned potatoes (no veg...).

Once, on an architecture field trip down the coast in Aberlady, I decided to run the 16 miles back to Edinburgh, having missed out on the Sunday run that week. This became a talking point in the alien culture of the architecture department and, when 'Aberlady' mutated into 'Aberfeldy' (although never 'Aberdeen') years later at New Town dinner parties, I kept my mouth shut. Without any effort on my part, the story had improved over time. However, the less said about the drunken post-race episodes which prevailed in our student days, the better.

I was a director of an architect's company in Edinburgh for many years, eventually retiring in 2016.

ALEX WIGHT

Alex Wight was from Duns and had a keen interest in sport from an early age, particularly cycling. Despite his diminutive stature, he was also captain of the school Under 15 rugby team but found that he was most successful at running and, for want of a bike, took up athletics, training for and competing in the school half mile and mile, and in handicap events around the Scottish Borders. He recalls being at the Edinburgh Highland Games at Murrayfield as a primary age schoolboy in 1952, when many of the competitors from the Helsinki Olympics were competing, and Jim Peters, who was the first man to run the marathon in under 2 hours 20 minutes, stands out as a hero of the day[51].

---

[51] The unfortunate Peters is best known for his roles in the 1952 Olympic and 1954 Empire Games marathons as a result of his dramatic defeats after he had started out as favourite in both events.

Alex came to Edinburgh in 1960 when the influence of the feats of Adrian Jackson, who had just left Edinburgh University to become a consultant anaesthetist, still lingered strongly. The EUHH club was dominated by senior 'medics' at the time and the new intake in 1960 included Tony Yates who was from Gordon Pirie's club, South London Harriers. Alex studied Mathematics and Natural Philosophy, and later completed a PhD in Computer Science.

In his first and second years he was hampered by constant injuries but he made the team for the Hyde Park Relay in 1961-62, where he saw the legendary Herb Elliott competing for his Cambridge college. Alex was a stalwart of the EUHH second team during this period, finishing second in the Scottish Universities second team championships in February 1962. Although he ran the first leg of the Edinburgh to Glasgow in 1962-63, progress through the next two seasons was slower than he would have wanted but by 1964-65 he was clear of injuries and won the Scottish Universities second team event in 1965. The regular training with the likes of Fergus Murray and Chris Elson, and increased mileage, started to pay off and by the 1965-66 season he had left grass tracks far behind and was a consistent member of the EUHH first team. He was in the winning EUHH teams in the Edinburgh to Glasgow in 1965 and 1966, the Scottish National Championships in 1966, 1967 (when he was second counter for the team) and 1968, and the Scottish Universities, the British Universities Championships and the Hyde Park Relay in 1967.

However, Alex was mainly interested in road racing, including the Morpeth to Newcastle and longer distance events in Scotland, and in April 1966 he ran his first marathon at Beverley in Yorkshire, finishing second in 2:23:15, while a resident at 'The Zoo' in Morningside. This was a huge breakthrough ('the future had been glimpsed...') and confirmation that by dint of continuing hard work he could be a serious contender at UK level in marathon and ultra events. Alex also entered distance running folklore around this time when, after being away all day on a lecture course, he went out at midnight on his return to 'The Zoo' in Morningside and put in a 15 mile run on the Edinburgh streets. His training diary at the time fails to verify exactly to which day the run was allocated.

His potential at the longer distances on the road was more than fulfilled when he won the Edinburgh to North Berwick 22 mile race in 1967 by six minutes in 2:02:15, missing the record by just 25 seconds, and later on, as a member of Edinburgh Athletic Club, the Two Bridges Race over 36 Miles between the Kincardine and Forth Road crossings in 1971 and 1972, the latter in a course record time. The Edinburgh to North Berwick was extended to the marathon distance and in 1971 he won in 2:15:27 from his brother Jim (2:15:43). It was to rank him fifth in the UK for the marathon that year, and he is still listed in the top 150 UK marathon performers of all time.

A typical week's training in 'The Zoo' years was:

Sunday – 21 miles on the Pentlands; **Monday** – 10 miles; **Tuesday** - 15 miles; **Wednesday** - 10 miles *fartlek* with the EUHH team; **Thursday** – 10 miles; **Friday** – 5 miles easy; **Saturday** – Race or 10 miles

Four or five additional sessions of up to 5 miles, scattered throughout the week, gave him a total mileage of approximately 100.

He competed for Britain in a 25 kilometre road race in Helsinki in May 1972, finishing sixth behind Seppo Tuominen of the host country, who broke Ron Hill's course record. Lasse Viren, who went on to win the Olympic 5,000 and 10,000 metres titles later that year, finished third. Alex also represented Britain in a 10,000 metre road race in Koblenz in 1973. However, not all his representative success was on the road. He ran for Scotland in various cross country events including the matches against the Army and Scottish Universities and narrowly missed out on selection for the International Cross Country Championships in 1975 after finishing eighth in the 'Scottish'. On the track he ran three miles in 13:58.8 in August 1968 and, in 1973, 29:38.0 for 10,000 metres in the Scottish trials for the 1974 Commonwealth Games, which was not far short of selection for the Games.

Alex enjoyed the fact that a solo pursuit like running could be married so successfully with the team environment at EUHH and this was epitomised, in later years, by the world record 1 mile relay over 24 hours to which he and his brother Jim were major contributors for Edinburgh Athletic Club in 1974. Looking back, with his esoteric wit and observations, Alex finds the glow of his successes, however imperfectly recalled, a stark contrast to the pragmatic entries in his training diaries which tend to record too much about injuries, loss of form and excessively hard training.

Alex Wight retired in 2004 from Edinburgh University where he was a lecturer in the School of Informatics and Associate Dean for Admissions in the College of Science and Engineering.

CHRIS ELSON

Chris came from Rotherham where he was a young teammate at the local harriers of the former British mile record holder, Alan Simpson. As a result, when he arrived in Edinburgh in 1961, influenced by Bannister, Cerutty and Lydiard, he already knew a fair bit about training and coaching. Unfortunately, he found it difficult to integrate with the Edinburgh regime of the time as the hierarchy were suspicious of his approach to training, accusing him of taking the sport too seriously. However, Chris persisted and became a key member of the team for several years, and an important mentor for new and improving runners. He was at Edinburgh for seven years, gaining a BSc in Bacteriology and a PhD in Immunology, which he continued to teach into his late sixties on a part time basis at Bristol University where he was Emeritus Professor and a revered mentor to students.

He initially fitted running round his course work but, after working hard until his first exam, when he established himself as one of the top students in his year, he managed to achieve a good balance between studies and sport. From the outset at Edinburgh he was one of the leading runners in the EUHH team finishing well up in East District events and winning his first inter-varsity match against St Andrews. However, he still remains bitter about the condescending attitude of the EUHH committee in the early 1960s, some of whom considered training more than three or four times a week almost tantamount to cheating, and he was deprived of his Blue in his first year. It would have been a great comfort to him to have younger athletes of the calibre and dedication of Fergus Murray and Alex Wight as teammates, receptive to his ideas and willing to push themselves in training at the time.

His best performance on the track while at Edinburgh was his victory in the 1964 East District mile (an event he first won as a first year student) in 4:10.9, ahead of Fergus Murray. In the Edinburgh to Glasgow Relay, which he competed in six times, he set a new record on the eighth leg in 1966, when EUHH recorded the second of their three successive wins. At cross country, he was second in the East Districts in 1963, when the team finished second, and second again (just 2 seconds behind Bill Ewing of Aberdeen) in 1966, the team winning comprehensively on that occasion.

Chris was also second scorer (behind Fergus Murray) for the EUHH team which won the Scottish Junior Championships in 1963 and was in the winning team at the Scottish Universities in 1965 (finishing 3rd individual) and 1966 (6th), the Hyde Park Relay in 1966, the Scottish

Senior Championships in 1967 and the British Universities in the same year. His selection for the British Universities Championships in 1967 came about when, the previous week, after recovering from illness, he won the Scottish Universities second team championships in a time which corresponded to fifth in the first team race in which Edinburgh had the first eight finishers.

Unfortunately, constant attacks of flu and hay fever took their toll and prevented him from reaching the levels of achievement as a young athlete which his talent deserved. He rates his all-time best performance as a handicap race at the unlikely Clay Cross Miners Gala in 1964, when he ran 3:46.0 off 120 yards, which equates to around 4:02 for the mile.

A typical week's training at his peak consisted of:

Sunday - 21 miles steady; **Monday** – Lunchtime 8 mile *fartlek*, evening steady run; **Tuesday** - 13-14 miles steady; **Wednesday** - 10 mile *fartlek* with club; **Thursday** - 13-14 miles steady; **Friday** – Easy jog if racing or 7-8 miles *fartlek*; **Saturday** - Race or 10 mile *fartlek*.

Total mileage for week – c. 80 to 90.

In many ways Chris Elson best illustrated his potential in reverse by running at the top UK level as an M60 veteran athlete when, finally free of illness, he led the rankings with a time of 4:44.1 for 1,500 metres in 2002. His other times as a 'vet' include 31:19 for 10,000 metres at age 40, 50:48 for ten miles at 41, 9:29 for 3,000 metres at 55 and 16:53 for 5,000 metres at age 57. He is still running today, in his mid-70s, and coaches young athletes at Bristol and West Athletics Club.

DAVE LOGUE

Dave Logue came over to Edinburgh from the Royal Belfast Academical Institution in 1965 at the age of 19. He was different from most of the other runners, big, extrovert and upbeat, definitely not a shrinking violet. He was six feet three tall which was unusual in itself for a distance runner, in the mould of Jack Batcheler, the American marathon runner, or his boyhood hero, and later international team mate, Derek 'Big D' Graham of the Ninth Old Boys Club in Belfast.

Dave first fell for athletics when he read about Ron Delany of Ireland winning the Olympic 1,500 metres in Melbourne in 1956, and watched the grainy TV footage of Derek Ibbotson setting a world mile record at the White City, London in 1957. The Rome Olympic Games in 1960, where Elliott, Snell and Halberg, and the often forgotten double silver medallist Hans Grodotzki of Germany, were in the starring roles, was another fondly remembered influence. Later on the die was further cast when, eschewing rugby which he loved but was just not the right build for, he won the school's junior cross country in 1960. Water Polo vied with running for his attention for a time but he joined North Belfast Harriers in 1963 and started training regularly that year.

His career ambitions were directed into veterinary science and it was the stories of the runners from Edinburgh, including Fergus Murray and Chris Elson, who had come over to Belfast and trounced Queen's University at cross country, which made up his mind in opting for Edinburgh over other vet schools in Scotland and England. He had represented Northern Ireland in the mile at the Schools International in 1965, finishing fourth behind another future EUHH runner, Jack Macfie, in 4:25.8. At Edinburgh he was on the cusp of the first team from day one, and gained a 'Green' in his first year.

Dave became a regular in the EUHH first team from his second year and was a member of the winning team in the Scottish Junior Cross Country Championships in 1967 (fifth in the individual) and the Senior in 1968 (13th). He ran the fourth leg for the winning teams at the Edinburgh to Glasgow Relay in 1966 and 1967. In University competition he was a member of the Edinburgh teams which won the Scottish Universities in 1966, 1967, 1968 and 1969, the British Universities in 1967 and the Hyde Park Relay in the same year. Individually while at Edinburgh he was third in the Scottish Universities in 1967 and won it in 1968 and 1970. He was captain of the EUHH team in season 1968-69 and finished fifth in the individual event that year, having been directed off-course at Heriot Watt University when in the lead.

After graduating from Edinburgh in 1970, Dave embarked on a PhD at Glasgow University and, after initially running for fun, started to take training seriously again, often in the company of his friend Colin Youngson, Aberdeen University graduate and later a three-time Scottish marathon champion, who was teaching in Glasgow at the time, and competing for Victoria Park AAC. Before long, Dave went on to even greater success including another individual victory in the Scottish Universities in 1974 and first place in the Midland (later West) District Cross Country Championships in the same year. Competing for Glasgow University in

1973, he ran the sixth stage of the Edinburgh to Glasgow faster than Ian Stewart, finishing just 16 seconds behind Andy McKean's record breaking run. He was also individual winner of the annual Scottish Universities versus Scottish Cross Country Union match in 1973 and 1974, the latter when representing Northern Ireland which had been invited to compete for the first time.

He suffered from exostosis to his knees and damaged Achilles tendons during his running career and, as a result, achieved many of his better performances when he was quite a bit older, and clear of injury, including victory in the Northern Ireland Cross Country Championships in 1974 and third in the 'Scottish' in 1977, running for Edinburgh Southern Harriers. He represented Northern Ireland in the International Cross Country Championships six times between 1968 and 1976.

On the track, while still at Edinburgh University, Dave set a Northern Ireland record of 9:06.6 for the 3,000 metres steeplechase in 1970 and was selected for the Commonwealth Games in Edinburgh that year. However, his best performances were at 5,000 metres, particularly at the Scottish Championships at Meadowbank each year, including a 14:04.0 clocking in June 1974 and 14:05.8 in 1975. He also ran 8:05.2 for 3,000 metres at Cwmbran in 1975. In 1977, at the age of 30, he achieved a significant and long deserved breakthrough to 13:53.0 for 5,000 metres in the Scottish Championships and set another personal best, of 29:03.8 for 10,000 metres, in winning GRE Gold Cup (for British club teams) for Edinburgh Southern in Cwmbran in September of that year. He and Allister Hutton, future London Marathon winner, ran many successful British League races together for Edinburgh Southern in the mid-1970s.

His ideal weekly mileage was 60, including a long run of 15 miles or so on the Sunday and he alternated between hard, including *fartlek*, medium and easy days for the rest of the week. He had a reputation for his gruelling training sessions but his most enjoyable runs were always the more relaxed, easy ones with his pals.

Dave was renowned for his outgoing personality and team members recall looking on with a mixture of amusement, admiration and downright embarrassment as he 'entertained' the crowd with the 'Wild Rover', and other 'favourites', as they awaited the results of the Scottish National Championships at Hamilton Racecourse in 1968. There are also rumours that he learned his water jumping technique by running over cars after ten pints of beer on a Saturday night. He was a principal component of many of EUHH's successes but he rates the third place in the Edinburgh to Glasgow, which the team managed in 1969, as the most satisfying because it was achieved, against the odds, by the runt of the great team of the mid 1960s.

Dave Logue is Emeritus Professor and Honorary Senior Research Fellow at Glasgow University Veterinary School. He lives in Ayr, and still enjoys regular runs with friends.

IAIN HATHORN

Iain Hathorn's interest in cross country running originated at Sedbergh School in Cumbria where, after his earlier schooling in his home town of Stranraer, he was a boarder from the age of fourteen until he went to Edinburgh to study Dentistry in 1963.

At school, running was a useful outlet for the games masters on days when the principal sports of rugby and cricket were postponed due to the weather. Iain discovered on these occasions that he had a natural aptitude for the sport and he won school colours for his successes in the Wilson Run, an annual ten mile fell race held in March each year, finishing a revelatory sixth in 1962 and third in 1963. He still kicks himself for the lack of self-belief that he feels might have cost him at least a runner-up spot in his final year. Regardless of the fluctuations in weather and conditions it is remarkable that his time from 1963 of 1:14:55 would have won the Wilson Run as recently as 2014, over 50 years later.

However, Iain did not appear to have much interest in the wider sport of athletics until he went to Edinburgh University. Running was to be a hobby which he would dabble in until graduation and he was not as driven, at least in the early years, as some of the others in the EUHH team. As a result he was happy to compete for the second team at first, in the company of Brian Covell, Chris Lord and others, and he didn't take training particularly seriously until the end his third year. However, during the University vacation in the summer of 1966, Iain competed in the annual Ben Nevis race held in August and finished 21st on his 21st birthday, completing the course from Fort William to the summit and back in under two hours. The progress he made through training for this race was a revelation to him, and it gave him the grounding to have a serious 'go' at the sport for his final two years at Edinburgh, resulting in him being awarded his 'Blue' in 1967 and 1968.

Early in season 1966-67 he ran the fastest leg in the East District Cross Country Relays, finishing ahead of John Linaker, who was one of the leading runners in Scotland at the time. As a track half miler the shorter cross country distance of two and a half miles suited him and this gave him a further boost in confidence and the reward of a place in the Scottish team for the annual match against the Army.

By this time Iain was an established member of the formidable EUHH first team, and in November of 1966, competing in the event for the first time, he set the fastest ever time on the third leg of the Edinburgh to Glasgow Relay as the team obliterated the event record and ran out easy winners for the second year running. This was achieved ahead of the great Motherwell YMCA Harriers team, which had won this classic road relay in 1962, 1963 and 1964. In the same season Iain was a member of the winning team at the British Universities Championships and finished sixth in the Scottish Universities, won by Ian Young. He also added to his fell running credentials with a record breaking victory in the EUHH Arthur's Seat Race in 1967.

Inspired by the careers of world class runners like Jim Alder and Peter Snell, Iain spent some time as a boarder at 'The Zoo', the rented house of runners in Morningside, where he trained with Fergus Murray, Roger Young, Chris Elson, Alex Wight and Alistair Matson. Dental studies continued to take precedence but he managed 60 miles a week in training for a period, and still found time to be one of the main protagonists when it came to the EUHH social side of things. One of his memorable performances was that of an acrobatic choirmaster (to chants of '60 miles a week, 60 miles a week....') on the bus back from Durham after the team had annihilated the opposition in a university cross country race in the mid-1960s.

From 1965 to 1967, Iain took on the important role of secretary of the Club, dealing with all the travel arrangements and correspondence and earning the monikers of 'Hatman' (which stuck) and 'Mathers', other people's reading of his barely decipherable signature.

On the track he was Edinburgh University champion over 880 yards in 1968, by inches, after an epic battle with Jack Macfie, and ran 14:29 for the three miles in the same year. He was also pacey enough to finish second in the Scottish Universities 440 yards in 1966 and he finished third in the 880 yards at the same championships in 1967. He represented Scottish Universities and the East District at 880 yards in 1968 and had a best time for the distance of 1:54.3. Iain spent a year competing for

Edinburgh Athletic Club after graduation, even winning the club sprint championships, but thereafter he took up (mostly recreational) rugby and, much to his later regret, from the age of 24 never trained seriously or competed in athletics again.

There is no doubt that this talented athlete could have achieved success at international level in the sport if he had been as ambitious as some of his EUHH team mates. But sport was never as important as his career and he often found training tedious and difficult to take seriously despite the great sense of well-being he got from being extremely fit.

Iain Hathorn retired from his post as a Consultant Orthodontist at Bristol University in 2006 and was Chairman of the British Orthodontic Society from 2006 to 2009. He still lives in Bristol and continues to enjoy enduring friendship with his old EUHH and EUAC team mates.

* * *

The Support Runners

WILLIE ALLAN

A pedigree in the long jump was responsible in part for Willie Allan's long career in athletics. His father, a great supporter and mentor, was the Inter-Scholastic Games (the precursor of the Scottish Schools Championships) long jump champion in 1915 and Willie himself was a successful jumper, being a regular winner at Lockerbie and Dumfries Academy school sports. He emulated his father's achievement by winning the Scottish Schools Under-17 triple jump championship in 1962. But significantly Willie's heroes were all runners, including Eric Liddell, whose story he read as a youngster, Chris Chataway, Peter Snell and Herb Elliott. He recalls in particular watching the Chataway versus Kuts race in the London-Moscow meeting at the White City in 1954 on television. Co-incidentally, Willie competed in one of the last ever races at the iconic old stadium, running 9:13.8 off scratch in the steeplechase at the London Fire Brigade Sports in August 1969.

Agricultural Science studies took precedence over sport in his first year at University, but a chance meeting with Alistair Matson in Edinburgh in the summer of 1964 resulted in him joining up with the Hare and Hounds for the annual autumn training camp, then at Cockburnspath. The result was over fifty years of training and competition, including a very successful later career as a veteran athlete.

Willie's time at Edinburgh coincided exactly with the most successful years in the club's history but, with a dedicated approach to training, he developed over three years from an overweight former long jumper to a very successful long distance runner, often representing the first team. In his final year he represented Scottish Universities and was one of seven members of the EUHH team to gain a Blue in cross country. Such was the standard at Edinburgh that Willie would have been the leading athlete in many of the other Scottish club sides at the time. He also had the unique distinction of running in the British Universities Championships in 1967 for Scottish Universities (in a conterminous match against the English equivalent, the Universities Athletics Union) having just missed out on selection for the Edinburgh team which went on to win the team race.

He won several honours in cross country and road team competition while at Edinburgh. These included victory in the Scottish Junior Championships and the Edinburgh to Glasgow Road Relay in 1965 (where he was third fastest individual on the third leg), third place in the Scottish Junior Championships in 1966, first in the Scottish Universities Championships in 1967, and first in the Scottish Senior Championships in the same year. Willie's main event on the track was the steeplechase, in which he was Surrey champion in 1970, and he had a best time of 9:13.0, set at the Scottish Championships in 1968.

After graduating in 1967 Willie moved to England and went on to have a very successful career as a veteran runner, winning many honours including the British Masters Athletics Federation M60 Ten Miles in 2005, the BMAF M70 half marathon in 2015 and the London Marathon M60 in 2006. He was the top M60 marathon runner in the UK that year, with a time of 2:55:42. He had many other successes at international veteran level and represented England, having eschewed Scotland due to selection issues, many times at cross country. He ran a 3:18:06 marathon at the age of 69 in 2014.

At his peak Willie ran 80-90 miles a week in training. This included a long run of 16-plus miles on a Sunday, two fartlek sessions a week and twice daily training on five days. As an M60 vet his mileage was in the region of 40-45 miles a week, with increased workload in the build up to a marathon, including a 20 mile Sunday run.

Looking back he is conscious of the importance of balancing fitness and injury. Better to err on the cautious side and avoid an injury than try to train through it in the hope it will go away. The downsides of training too hard, and too little in the way of tapering off for important races, were lessons he learnt through experience but the benefits of training he feels are eventually limited by genetic potential in any case. However, he is very much aware of the sense of well-being and confidence engendered by the feeling of fitness, and the camaraderie of like-minded people. Sadly, the monitoring of doping, with the attendant need to be available for random testing, has, even at super veteran level, been a bugbear of his later running career.

Despite all the obsessive dedication and hard work, Willie saw the funny side of athletics too, and recalls many evenings boring 'lay' company, including his future wife Glennis, talking about running with his pals all night in the pub. The washing of foul smelling running kit was also a source of amusement, and Willie was known to wind other runners up by shouting 'goan yersel' at them from a passing car (in the company of an audience of appreciative fellow athletes), especially when it was windy and pouring with rain.

Willie Allan gained an Open University Business School MBA at the age of 45 and, after having previously worked for a number of multi-national companies in the agricultural supplies business, he set up and ran a very successful company in agricultural engineering, and later agricultural chemicals, trading in many parts of Europe and the USA.

ALISTAIR MATSON

Alistair Matson (affectionately known as 'The Bomb') studied law at Edinburgh from 1962 to 1966, and was responsible for obtaining the lease to 'The Zoo' at 78 Morningside Drive in Edinburgh in 1965 where, along with Fergus Murray and company, he clocked up prodigious distances on the nearby roads and hills. He recalls running at school in Abingdon, first at sprints and later at longer distances, inspired by the rivalries between Chataway and Kuts, and Bannister and Landy, and particularly by the 1956 Olympics in Melbourne. His school concentrated on rugby in the winter and cricket in the summer but an enthusiastic master joined the staff and started up a cross country team which was active in the Easter term. Alistair was encouraged to try longer runs on the roads and country, and enjoyed the pressure-free environment of the countryside.

He was 'blown away' by the options for activities when he arrived in Edinburgh and even played cricket in his first year. But he soon joined the Hare and Hounds and decided to concentrate on running which offered such satisfaction in its direct correlation between what you put in to training and what you got out of it. By 1964 he was running up to 40 to 50 miles a week, going on to 60/70 by the time he left University and rising to 70/80 by 1969 when he was still resident in Edinburgh and competing for Edinburgh Southern Harriers. By this time a typical week's training (from 20-26 April 1969), consisted of:

> **Sunday** – 21.5 miles steady on road; **Monday** – a.m. 3.5miles jog; p.m. 8miles *fartlek*/interval running on grass; **Tuesday** – 10.5 miles steady on road; **Wednesday** – a.m. 5 miles steady on beach and golf course; p.m. 7 miles interval running; **Thursday** - a.m. 4miles easy *fartlek* on grass; p.m. 5 miles strides; **Friday** – 3.5miles easy jog grass; 4 miles easy strides grass; **Saturday** - TRACK RACE: Edinburgh Southern Harriers Club Championships 6 miles – 2nd in 30min 20secs (Cinder track at Fernieside - 5 laps to mile).

Total mileage for week – c. 80

At EUHH he featured in the first team from time to time and was in the team which won the Scottish Senior Cross Country Championships in 1966. His road racing debut was in the Brampton to Carlisle '10' in 1964 where he recorded 53:40, a time which was extremely pleasing for a developing athlete in these days.

Although Alistair Matson's best competitive performances were on the road, he was fourth in the Scottish 10,000 metres track championships in 1969 in 30:56.8 and ran 14: 51.0 for 5,000 metres in the same year.

After a 2:43:18 marathon debut as a 22 year old at Shettleston in 1965 he went on to run 2:30:40 at the same event in May 1967. He ran 25 successive London Marathons and competed in many other marathons, half marathons and 20 mile events. Ultra running also features prominently in his CV and he competed in the Comrades Marathon over 56 miles in Durban, South Africa, the London to Brighton (54 miles), Woodford to Southend (40 miles) , the Two Bridges (36 miles) and some 100k road championships.

Like Willie Allan, Alistair was very successful at the veteran level and ran a 2 hour 40 minute marathon at the age of 48 in 1991. He was South East AA M60 champion at cross country in 2003. In addition to Edinburgh Southern Harriers, his clubs after EUHH included Wycombe Phoenix Harriers, Crawley Athletic Club and Lingfield Running Club.

His advice to aspiring runners is to keep as relaxed as possible when running, avoiding a style which is alien to your natural posture, and make sure you wear the right footwear. Aside from the euphoria of a good performance, running he feels is such a natural physical activity, a great, convenient and stress-reducing way to exercise when time is short. On the downside he feels that it can become too obsessive and can take over your life with constant analysing of progress, and planning of training and racing programmes, often leaving you too tired for other activities including a meaningful social life. The problem of having to adjust to reduced training or stopping entirely due to age or health issues can also be difficult for some people to deal with, and adjustment to diet and seeking of alternative physical activity after retirement from the sport can be vitally important.

Alistair Matson completed his qualifications as a solicitor in 1969 and, after a year living and working in Zimbabwe, he returned to the UK to work for the British Airports Authority at Heathrow for twenty years, and then in administrative posts with the NHS until his retirement in 2000.

* * *

The Legacy

Two athletes in particular stand out from the period following the BUSF victory in 1967, Andy McKean and Jim Dingwall.

ANDY MCKEAN

Andy McKean came to Edinburgh to study architecture in 1967, the season after the British Universities success, attracted in part by the exploits of Fergus Murray and his team mates, which gave Edinburgh University Architecture Department the edge over Cambridge. It took Andy a season or two to make his mark in the fiercely competitive running environment at Edinburgh but he went on to become one of the most successful domestic cross country runners Scotland has ever produced, winning the 'National' on four occasions, a record which has been surpassed by only three other athletes in the history of the sport.

However, partly through injury and partly through choice, he did not have the stellar track career which might have been expected of him and, perhaps because he didn't take track running very seriously, he never received the credit his brilliant record as a cross country runner really deserved. Nevertheless, he was British Universities 5,000 metres champion in 1970 and won the Scottish 10 Mile Track Championship in 1972.

He was born and grew up in London and attended Merchant Taylors School, where his brother Robert had shown considerable promise as an athlete (and later attended and ran successfully for St Andrews University), and found running an 'enjoyable activity' when the compulsory team sports were postponed due to the weather. Andy, whose mother had been a very successful sportsperson in her own right, was persuaded to 'give it a try' in the hope that he would display a similar aptitude to Robert. Although athletics and cross country running at Merchant Taylors, as in so many other schools, did not have the status of rugby and cricket, Andy was permitted to specialise and, having started to train regularly at the age of 16, he took part in competitive inter-scholastic matches and occasional more prestigious events such as the Hertfordshire Schools Championships, which he won in his final year at school.

He also joined Hillingdon AC at this time and ran for them in cross country and track events. The club coach, Andy Coe, introduced him to systematic training schedules including speedwork and mobility exercises, which complemented the steady running he was doing on his own, and became a regular part of his training regime. He ran the mile in 4:19.6 before leaving school in 1967.

As a slightly younger athlete than those of the 'Murray era', Andy's 'heroes' at the time were more contemporary than the likes of Gordon Pirie and Jim Peters, and he found inspiration from the performances of the exciting trio of Dick Taylor, Allan Rushmer and Ian McCafferty as well as those of Fergus Murray himself. Jim Hogan who, among many other successes won the European Marathon title in 1966, used to train barefoot on the playing fields at the school and was another great influence.

Edinburgh proved an inspired choice for running with plenty of training options on offer, including Holyrood Park, the University Gym in the Pleasance and King's Buildings, where the EUHH team set out from on their Wednesday training sessions. For both speed work and endurance, The Meadows and Bruntsfield Links, which were very close to Andy's flat in Lauriston Gardens, allowed for off-road training at night during the winter, thanks to the generous street lights.

Although Andy didn't take long to become a regular in the EUHH first team, and was captain of the club in 1969-70 and 1971-72, it was not until his intermediate 'year out' in an architect's office from 1970, the year of the Commonwealth Games in Edinburgh, that he was motivated to increase his weekly mileage significantly. The office job allowed him a more regular, less pressurised lifestyle than architectural course work, enabling him to fit in long evening training runs around more flexible meal times. This was the period of his real breakthrough and from 1970 to 1977 he ran at least 4,000 miles every year, at an incredible average of nearly 80 miles per week, every week for eight years. A typical week's training at his peak consisted of:

> **Sunday** - 20 miles steady; **Monday** - am 5 miles steady; pm 5 miles fartlek; **Tuesday** - am 8 miles steady; pm 5 miles interval work (track or grass); **Wednesday** - 10 miles fartlek plus 2 miles warm up/down; **Thursday** - am 5 miles steady; pm 5 miles fartlek; **Friday** - 5 miles slow steady; **Saturday** - 6 miles race plus 4 miles warm up/down.

> **Total mileage for week – c. 80.**

He also did mobility exercises every day as part of his warm up, both for training and for competition.

In March 1972, after finishing fourth in the 'Scottish', Andy ran for British Universities in the International Students Cross Country Championships, finishing fourth in that race and third counter for Britain, behind English Internationals Jack Lane and Andy Holden. He improved markedly the following season and went on to emulate Fergus Murray by winning both the British Universities and the Scottish National cross country titles in his final academic year in 1973, yet still found time to gain a first class honours in architecture. In the British Universities race, held at Guildford, he won by 20 seconds from Lane, who had taken the title over the same course in 1971.

After graduation, Andy joined Edinburgh Athletic Club for whom he won three further Scottish titles and finished third behind David Black and Bernie Ford at the English National Championships in Sheffield in 1974 where the nine miles of deep snow and mud at the aptly named Graves Park suited his running style perfectly. He also finished seventh in this prestigious event at Luton in 1975 and fifth at Leicester in 1976. These were major achievements for a Scottish-based runner and gave him a consistently superior career record to almost all of the great Scottish runners of the time.

In addition, he won the East District cross country title four times and set the record for the renowned sixth stage of the Edinburgh to Glasgow Relay, an event he graced on many occasions from 1967 until his retirement from the sport in 1978. A particular career highlight was his second place representing Britain in an international road race in Barcelona in 1975, just behind the late Bronislaw Malinowski of Poland (who went on to win the Olympic Steeplechase in 1980) and he also enjoyed considerable success in invitation cross country events in the 1970s, mixing it with the best runners in Europe at the time. He competed for Scotland eight times in the International Cross Country Championships and was captain of the Scottish team in 1977 in Dusseldorf, and again in Glasgow in 1978 where, despite having drastically reduced his training mileage prior to retiring from the sport, he had his best ever run in the event, finishing 19th.

Despite his single minded attitude to training and competition, Andy enjoyed the camaraderie of athletics and recalls good times with his friends and rivals at this time, including his teammates at EUHH as well as his rivals at other Scottish universities and clubs. Dave Logue was a useful mentor to him in the early years at Edinburgh and he trained regularly with the likes of Alex Wight and Jim Dingwall. His main adversaries in Scotland at the time of his heyday from season 1972-73 were Jim Brown of Monkland Harriers and Borough Road College, Adrian Weatherhead of Edinburgh Athletic Club, Nat Muir of Shettleston Harriers, winner of a record eight Scottish Senior Cross Country titles, and Allister Hutton of Edinburgh Southern Harriers, a two-time Scottish Cross Country Champion and winner of the London Marathon in 1990. All these athletes were British Internationalists on the track.

Andy McKean had a reputation for a relentless approach to both training and competition, often going straight to the front at the beginning of races and gradually pulling away from the opposition with his unforgiving, almost metronomic, even pace. This was never better illustrated than by his superb 46 second victory over the second-placed Adrian Weatherhead at the 'Scottish' in 1975. The doggedness grew out of his belief in the value of consistency in training over a period of years, rather than what he saw as vast weekly mileages or unduly hard or intensive workouts. What he regarded as 'conscious restraint' helped him avoid injuries and ensured a training plateau that could be maintained without interruption and, as far as possible, remained enjoyable.

This approach was in no small measure helped by his decision later on to eschew the track for what he referred to as 'active rest' over the summer months. But he still had time for a fairly wild social life revolving round the sport, where he rivalled the English steeplechaser Holden and his extrovert Welsh cohort Pete Griffiths, a Hillingdon AC clubmate, for his ability to down eight pints of beer, even puff on the occasional fag or two, and still be up and about for a 15 mile run the next morning.

For the record, his best track times were 14:12.5 for 5,000 metres, 29:40.2 for 10,000 metres and 49:25.8 for ten miles on the track, when winning the Scottish title in 1972.

Andy McKean worked primarily as a civil servant for the Scottish Office, retiring in the early 2000s, and now lives in Gatehouse of Fleet where he has a successful second career as a watercolourist.

JIM DINGWALL

With his staccato cadence and upright carriage (once described as 'looking as if he was carrying a tray of cakes') Jim Dingwall could never be characterised as the epitome of style but, from modest beginnings, he went on to become one of Scotland's greatest ever marathon runners and a prolific competitor worldwide. He was also blessed with one of the most devastating sprint finishes of his generation and was even rumoured to leave Lachie Stewart lost for pace in the home straight.

Jim began his athletics career as a sprinter at George Heriot's School in Edinburgh and was in the winning Heriot's team in the Scottish Schools (Under 15) 4 x 110 yards relay in 1964. He became more interested in longer distances in his later years at school and, much like Dave Logue but for different reasons, took up cross country running having forgone rugby, the sport everyone was expected to participate in at the time. He was gamely pursued on his *fartlek* sessions at Heriot's by his contemporary, Don Jamie, and by 1967, when he embarked on his fresher year in Chemistry at Edinburgh University, where he was to go on to complete his doctorate, Jim was well versed in mile and cross country training and competition.

However, he was not an immediate success with EUHH and competed for the second team for a year or two. He also ran for Heriot's Former Pupils Athletic Club in minor club events on the track in the summer, when opportunities arose. Although cross country was not his particular forte, primarily because the courses often did not suit his running style, Jim persevered with the training regime to which he was introduced at Edinburgh, and went on to gain his Cross Country Blue in 1969-70, 1971-72 and 1972-73 and his Athletics Blue in 1970-71 and 1972-73.

He was third in the Scottish Universities Cross Country Championships in 1972 and eighth the following year when the team won. His best performance in the British Universities was 34th place in 1973 at Guildford when Andy McKean won the individual race and the team finished a creditable sixth. Long after graduation, while competing for Falkirk Victoria Harriers, Jim did eventually achieve considerable success in this area of the sport finishing fourth in the Scottish National Senior Championships in 1979, sixth in 1983 and fifth (at the age of 35) in 1985. He competed for Scotland in the International Cross Country Championships in each of these years.

On the track Jim, in his irrepressible way, followed in the footsteps of Fergus Murray and Andy McKean by winning the British Universities 5,000 metres at Brighton in 1973, in a time of 14:12.8, illustrating his versatility and talent by finishing second in both the 1,500 metres and the 10,000 metres at the same championships over the same weekend. He went on to record times of 3:45.8 for 1,500 metres in May 1973, 7:57.8 for 3,000 metres (a Scottish Native and All Comers' record at the time) in June 1975, and 13:48.0 for 5,000 metres in the same year. In addition he was Scottish 10,000 metre champion on three occasions with a best time of 28:45.25, set in 1978.

His main successes, however, were achieved on the road and the seeds of his later achievements were evident as early as 1970 when he ran 13:58 for the first leg of the Hyde Park Relay as the team finished fourth. He was a hugely committed club runner and this was never better exemplified than by his performances in the Edinburgh to Glasgow Relay which he competed in five times for EUHH, once while with Edinburgh Athletic Club after graduation and 12 times for Falkirk Victoria Harriers, an astonishing total of 18 appearances all told. Individually he was fastest on the first leg for EUHH in 1971, eight seconds ahead of leading marathon man Bill Stoddart, fastest on the eighth leg for Edinburgh Athletic Club in 1974, fastest on the second leg for Falkirk in 1976, and equalled Andy McKean's prodigious record of 31:00 on the stellar sixth leg for Falkirk in 1977. Among many other road racing successes Jim won the Windermere to Kendal Road Race ahead of me in March 1975, and then again in 1976, biding his time and outsprinting Mike Freary in the steep downhill finish to the Town Hall in Kendal with me, helpless against his turn of pace, in third.

However, it was at the marathon that he achieved international success, winning the Scottish title in 1977 in a championship record of 2:16:05, which stood for 22 years. He represented Scotland at the Commonwealth Games in Edmonton, Canada in 1978, finishing 18th after running in the leading group with 10 miles to go before succumbing to illness. His best time was achieved in finishing fifth in the London Marathon in 1983 in 2:11:44, which remains the fifth fastest ever by a Scot and 38th in the UK all-time rankings. Altogether he ran in 54 marathons, winning races as far afield as France, Israel and Hong Kong, and completed 20 London Marathons from 1981 to 2003, the last four after recovering from serious illness. His time in 2003, aged 53, was 2:47:30.

Jim was a very sociable character, highly respected from his time at EUHH and beyond, being dubbed 'The Guv'nor', which reflected his status among his running contemporaries. Beyond the daily grind of training, copious beers were enjoyed and songs sung but he always managed to maintain a strong degree of decorum in his social life, and never strayed into schadenfreude or profanity.

Jim Dingwall died of cancer at the age of 56 in Hull in 2005. He was such a popular and revered club man that two road races were subsequently named after him – the Jim Dingwall Memorial 10k Road Race held by his former club Falkirk Victoria Harriers in Grangemouth, where he worked as a research chemist for British Petroleum for many years, in April each year, and the Jim Dingwall 10k held every October in the East Riding of Yorkshire, where he lived at the end of his working career.

* * *

THE OTHERS

It would be elitist and unfair not to mention other dedicated (and not so dedicated) athletes who contributed so much to the success and the team spirit of EUHH during the 1960s:

Sandy Cameron (Loyal cross country team player and 2:30 marathon man.)

Brian Covell (Resident of 'The Zoo', mathematics and medical graduate, unofficial team photographer, race walker, fell runner and archivist for the 'Bob Graham Round' in the Lake District.)

John Exley (Stalwart first team man in the late 60s.....later on a very successful veteran runner...)

Ken Fyfe (Another stalwart and secretary of EUHH after Iain Hathorn. Ken went to Heriot Watt to do a post graduate course in 1968 and won the Scottish Universities Cross Country title for them in 1969, after the leading runners, in a race which was coincidentally hosted by Heriot Watt, had gone off course.)

Rab Hendry (Character from Kirkcaldy – talented, but didn't train very seriously. After several years running for the second team Rab was appointed captain of EUHH in 1970-71. At the British Universities in Guildford in 1971, after he had watched the second team race over two laps of two and a half miles, Rab mistakenly assumed the first team race would be covering the same distance. After his usual lung-bursting and nausea-inducing sprint at the end of the two laps, he noticed everyone else carrying on running. It is to his eternal credit that he was overtaken by only one runner in the third lap...)

Chris Lord (Leading runner and mentor for the second team...)

Donald Macdonald (First team man and secretary in the early 60s.)

Jack Macfie (Captain of the Edinburgh University athletics team in 1969, and a tenacious half miler.)

John Meldrum (Medical student who lived in 'The Zoo' and was the subject of the apocryphal tale of the runner sent out at midnight on a Saturday to take the week's mileage for the household up to the 600 mark.)

Dave Orr (A regular first team runner who, like Martin Sinclair, was an accomplished half miler on less than dedicated training.)

Martin Sinclair (Talented half miler renowned for his ability to win races on very little training.)

Hugh Stevenson (An impostor perhaps, being a hurdler and high jumper in 'real life', but a welcome one given the entertainment value he brought with him to EUHH social life. Captain of the athletics team in 1968 and winner of the 'Style Prize' at many Edinburgh University Sports.)

Dave Taylor (Dedicated distance runner, 2:30 marathon man, EUHH office bearer, party goer...)

John Blair-Fish, Gareth Buffet, Mike Casey, Robert Clark, Rod Combe, Doug Glover, Sandy Hardie, Brian Jamieson, Tegwyn Jones, Ian Kerr, Ian Malcolm, Ian Marshall, Alex Pattison, Eric Stevenson, Steve Taylor, Dave Watson, Doug Wood.....and many others whose names, with sincere apologies, have slipped from the memory.

POSTSCRIPT

One of the great mysteries about athletics in Scotland in recent years is how, 50 years on from the heyday of Edinburgh University Hare and Hounds, the overall standard of middle and long distance running at the upper level has not improved significantly. This is a pattern which seems to be played out in every Western society. Internationally records have been comprehensively rewritten, primarily by African runners but with one or two notable exceptions such as Mo Farah and Paula Radcliffe, while more people than ever compete in running events. However, Fergus Murray's best times for 5,000 metres on (mostly) cinder tracks between the years of 1963 and 1975 (1968 excepted) would have ranked him first in Scotland in six of the ten years between 2007 and 2016 and Gareth Bryan-Jones' time of 8:33.8 for the 3,000 metres Steeplechase, set in 1970, would have been top of the rankings in eight of these years.

In the 'good old days' everyone held down day jobs, there was none of the 'gear' (treadmills, heart monitors, specialised clothing, water bottles, MP3 players, oxygen tents) that there is today, you ate what you liked - monitoring for health and performance didn't exist[52], and shoes were heavier and much less comfortable – blisters were a constant problem.

Running tracks are much faster and more consistent now – grass and cinders required constant maintenance which wasn't always forthcoming, marathons were run without water, everyone was truly amateur in spirit (with the exception of the 'pedestrians' and those who indulged, for little benefit as it transpired, in dodges of the 'brown envelope' variety). Across the board there were stories of broken bottles in the water jump, concrete surrounds to the pole vault, high jump pits of sand, discus circles with no protection being used during track events.

So what are the issues which make the sport different today?

The teachers' strikes in the 1980s, which resulted in the rapid decline of school sports and inter-scholastic competition, especially in state schools, is a major cause, although this was not the fault of the teachers, more the lack of priority and funding given to extra-curricular activities. Before then, the school was a community where the captain of the rugby team or the skilful winger at football, or indeed the winner of the school mile, was looked up to and revered. Nowadays, 30 year old shots and

---

[52] Dave Logue once said that one of the great advantages of training so much was that you could eat and drink what you liked, without putting on weight!

discuses and hurdles (at least those which haven't already been recycled) lie rusting in school storage facilities, with Health and Safety concerns often blamed for their regrettable obsolescence.

Ironically, the jogging boom which originated in the late 1970s on the west coast of America and soon headed east to Europe, is also a factor, as it changed the purpose and image of running into something that was good for your mental and physical well-being - the Sri Chimnoy philosophy - but which was nevertheless quite the opposite of the fiercely competitive sport it had once been. This movement coincided with the gym culture where narcissism could be added to the mix. The idea of the average jogger today espousing the ideals of Lydiard and Cerutty is difficult to imagine.

With the advent of mass participation, the club scene, where runners trained together, shared ideas and enjoyed the camaraderie of the sport, began to decline. Everyone started to do their own thing. Runners generally still tried hard in races, but they didn't train to the same degree and their ambitions were much more modest. There were lots more races and events to enter but runners were more interested in improving their own best times on the road, almost regardless of what others were doing, than competing on the track or on the country. Why put yourself through a steeplechase or a muddy nine miles over plough when you could run a pleasant 10k on a level surface, wearing the latest ultra-light trainers with added bounce and a perfect fit, as you coast to another personal best time of 40 minutes?

Nowadays, in sports such as swimming, and particularly cycling, where athletes are confined to a specialised training facility (the pool and the track), the ruling bodies are able to control the development of elite squads in a holistic manner, in a 'laboratory' environment and in a training centre such as British Cycling's base in Manchester, where everything is monitored and managed to the utmost degree. Athletics, and long distance running in particular, has always had at least some flexibility in where and how to train but many individual athletes can be reduced to automatons, the physical machines through which their coach's ideas are fed. The result is that the standard of performances at the top level is much better than it used to be, but there is a considerable gap to the 'also rans', those who have missed out or who steadfastly avoid being controlled in this way.

To many promising young runners this must have a negative effect except for those who have ambitions at the highest elite level. The image of the lifestyles of great athletes like Radcliffe and Farah (run/ice bath/ eat/sleep/run/core exercises/eat/sleep), where steak and dessert (no booze) is a wild night out and chocolate consumption is 'naughty', is at such extreme odds with the other pressures and influences of society today. This can alienate youngsters who want to be good at sport, and perhaps even achieve success internationally, but who don't want the baggage of too many intrusions into their lifestyles.

But there is hope. By 2016 Scottish distance running, through the performances of Laura Muir, Andrew Butchart and Callum Hawkins, who had developed into world class athletes, and others at the elite level including Eilish McColgan, Chris O'Hare, Derek Hawkins and Steph Twell, was suddenly in the ascendancy again and these grounded role models pointed to an exciting future. Thanks to the approach of Scottish Athletics in promoting athletics through the clubs and at the grass roots level, rather than an elite model, clubs were thriving again, despite concerns about the lack of sufficient coaches to cope with increased participation. 647 runners completed the course in the men's Scottish National Senior Cross Country Championships in 2017 and 42 clubs contested the team race, with equally encouraging numbers in the women's event.

But a word too for older athletes in addressing Alistair Matson's concern about dealing with the loss of the 'high' of running after retirement from the sport. Thanks nowadays to changed attitudes to exercise and health generally, it is much more common for runners to continue training and to compete occasionally into their dotage and, heaven forbid, to enjoy it more than in their younger days when the pressure, which Gareth Bryan-Jones was referring to in his Athletics Weekly questionnaire, is at its greatest.

So why stop, if you don't need to and don't suffer (or perhaps do...) from major health issues or chronic injury? Chris Chataway, who could still run (but didn't have to) a 1:38:50 half marathon at the Great North Run on Tyneside at the age of 75 in 2006, summed it up perfectly when he referred to competitive running is his later years as 'Dixon of Dock Green replacing Joe Stalin'. Running without the extreme pressures of his twenties had become to him a 'friendly old codger'.

Happily, there are a few old codgers from the EUHH days of the 1960s still indulging in their lifelong obsession with distance running.

APPENDIX ONE

EUHH Team Achievements (1960 to 1970)

Scottish National Senior Cross Country Champions 1966, 1967, 1968
Scottish National Junior Cross Country Champions 1963, 1964, 1965, 1967
East of Scotland Cross Country Champions 1965, 1966, 1968
Edinburgh to Glasgow Road Relay Winners 1965, 1966, 1967
Hyde Park Relay Winners 1966, 1967, 1968
East District Cross Country Relay Winners 1966, 1967, 1968, 1969
Scottish Universities Cross Country Champions 1961, 1963, 1965, 1966, 1967, 1968, 1969
British Universities Cross Country Champions 1967 (Runners-up 1968)

APPENDIX TWO

EUHH Individual Achievements (1960-1970)

Winners of the East District Championships:

Adrian Jackson	1957, 1958, 1959
	1961 (while with Braidburn AC)
Fergus Murray	1964, 1965
Gareth Bryan-Jones	1968
Alistair Blamire	1970
Andy McKean	1973,
	1974, 1977, 1978 (while with Edinburgh Athletic Club)

Winners of the Scottish Universities Championships:

Adrian Jackson	1954, 1957, 1958, 1959
Fergus Murray	1964, 1965, 1966
Ian Young	1967
Dave Logue	1968, 1970
	1974 (while with Glasgow University Hares and Hounds)
Ken Fyfe	1969 (while with Heriot Watt University)
Alistair Blamire	1971
Andy McKean	1973

Winners of the British Universities Championships:

Fergus Murray	1964, 1966
Andy McKean	1973

Winners of the Scottish National Championships:

Fergus Murray	1964 (competing for Dundee Hawkhill Harriers), 1965, 1966
Andy McKean	1973
	1975, 1976, 1977 (while with Edinburgh Athletic Club)

APPENDIX THREE

EUHH Individual Honours (1960 to 1970)

Represented Scotland in the International Cross Country Union/International Amateur Athletics Federation Senior Championships:

Adrian Jackson	1958, 1959
	1961 (while with Braidburn Athletic Club)
Martin Craven	1963
Fergus Murray	1964, 1965, 1966
	1969, 1971 (while with Edinburgh Southern Harriers)
Roger Young	Selected in 1965 but withdrew from the team
Alistair Blamire	1967, 1968, 1971
	1972 (while with Shettleston Harriers)
	1974 (while with Edinburgh Southern Harriers)
Gareth Bryan-Jones	1968
	1969, 1970 (while with Edinburgh Southern Harriers)
Andy McKean	1971, 1972, 1973
	1974, 1975, 1976, 1977, 1978 (while with Edinburgh Athletic Club)
Jim Wight	1972 (while with Edinburgh Athletic Club)
Jim Dingwall	1979, 1983, 1985 (while with Falkirk Victoria Harriers)

Represented Northern Ireland in the International Cross Country Union/ International Amateur Athletics Federation Senior Championships:

Dave Logue	1968, 1969, 1970
	1973, 1974 (while with Glasgow University Hares and Hounds)
	1976 (while with Edinburgh Southern Harriers)

Represented Scotland in the International Cross Country Union Junior Championships:

Ian Young   1964 (while with Springburn Harriers)
                         1965
Alistair Blamire   1966

Represented Great Britain in the Olympic Games:

Fergus Murray   1964 (10,000 metres) (Tokyo)
Gareth Bryan-Jones   1968 (3,000 metres Steeplechase) (Mexico City)

Represented Scotland in the Commonwealth Games:

Fergus Murray   1966 (3 miles/6 miles) (Kingston, Jamaica)
                         1970 (Marathon) (while with Edinburgh Southern
                         Harriers)
Gareth Bryan-Jones   1970 (3,000 metres Steeplechase) (Edinburgh)
                         (while with Edinburgh Southern Harriers)
Jim Wight   1974 (Marathon) (Christchurch) (while with
                         Edinburgh Athletic Club)
Jim Dingwall   1978 (Marathon) (Edmonton) (while with Falkirk
                         Victoria Harriers)

Represented Northern Ireland in the Commonwealth Games:

Dave Logue   1970 (3,000 metres Steeplechase) (Edinburgh)

Represented Great Britain at Track and Field:

Fergus Murray   1964, 1965 (5,000 metres/10,000 metres)
                         1967 (10,000 metres) (while with Oxford University)
Gareth Bryan-Jones   1968 (3,000 metres Steeplechase)
                         1970 (3,000 metres Steeplechase) (while with
                         Edinburgh Southern Harriers)
Alistair Blamire   1969 (3,000 metres Steeplechase)

Represented Great Britain at Road Running:

Fergus Murray
Martin Craven (while with Kendal AAC)
John Batchelor (while with Ilford AC)
Alex Wight (while with Edinburgh Athletic Club)

Andy McKean (while with Edinburgh Athletic Club)

Represented British Universities:

Adrian Jackson, Fergus Murray, Chris Elson, Alistair Blamire, Dave Logue, Andy McKean.

Represented Scottish Universities:

Adrian Jackson, Mike Flower, Martin Craven, Fergus Murray, Chris Elson, Gareth Evans, Roger Young, Frank Gamwell, Ian Young, Alistair Blamire, Gareth Bryan-Jones, Jim Wight, Alex Wight, Alistair Matson, Iain Hathorn, Dave Logue, Willie Allan, Andy McKean, Ken Fyfe (while with Heriot-Watt), Jim Dingwall.

APPENDIX FOUR

EUHH Individual Best Performances (Track and Field) (1960-1970)

(Performances while a member of Edinburgh University Athletic Club only)

800 metres	Martin Sinclair	1 minute 50.6 seconds* - Grangemouth, 24 June 1967
1,500 metres	Fergus Murray	3 minutes 48.0 seconds* - Enfield, 15 July 1964
	(Jim Dingwall	3 minutes 45.8 seconds - Meadowbank, Edinburgh, 26 May 1973)
3,000 metres	Fergus Murray	8 minutes 02.0 seconds* - Crystal Palace, London, 17 August 1965 (Jim Dingwall 7 minutes 57.8 seconds – Meadowbank, Edinburgh 17 June 1975)
5,000 metres	Fergus Murray	13 minutes 47.0 seconds* - Portsmouth, 7 August 1965
10,000 metres	Fergus Murray	29 minutes 10.4 seconds – White City, London, 11 September 1964 (Fergus Murray 28 minutes 43.2 seconds* - White City, London, 14 July 1967)
Ten Miles	Fergus Murray	48 minutes 41.0 seconds – Hurlingham, 11 April 1964 (Fergus Murray 47 minutes 45.2 seconds –

Hurlingham, 29 April 1967)

Marathon	Fergus Murray	2 hours 18 minutes 30 seconds - Glasgow, 15 May 1965 (Jim Dingwall 2 hours 11 minutes 44 seconds – London, 17 April 1983)
3,000 metres S'chase	Gareth Bryan-Jones	8 minutes 36.2 seconds - White City, London, 13 July 1968
	(Gareth Bryan-Jones	8 minutes 33.8 seconds – Meadowbank, Edinburgh, 23 July 1970)

*Denotes converted from imperial equivalent
Performances in brackets represent superior career best times by former EUHH athletes from the period 1960-1970.

ACKNOWLEDGEMENTS

Especial thanks to Fergus Murray for access to his meticulous training diaries, photographs, newspaper cuttings, year books and bound copies of the 'bible', Athletics Weekly, and for many a chat over a glass of wine or a cup of coffee.

Thanks also to Dave Logue, Alex Wight, Ian Young, Andy McKean, Chris Elson, Roger Young, Gareth Bryan-Jones, Willie Allan, Alistair Matson and Iain Hathorn for their reminiscences, to Brian McAusland, Marie Craven, Doug Gillon, Kit Campbell, Arnold Black, Dave Taylor, and Sandy Sutherland for assistance with specific facts and to Brian again, Graeme Orr and Graham McIndoe for assisting with and providing images.

On a more general level the Scottish Distance Running History website by Brian McAusland and Colin Youngson and, of course, Wikipedia have been invaluable sources of help.

For supportive feedback and comments, thanks to my wife Alison Blamire, my old running pal Donald Macgregor (who also kindly agreed to write the Foreword) and my niece Polly Mackenzie. My friends Jack Davidson and Ed Jones made sure the grammar was just that little bit more refined, and the hyperbole appropriately restrained, and they offered pertinent suggestions and advice on content, and the nuances of publishing.

BIBLIOGRAPHY

Books:

Harold Abrahams (Presenter), 'XVII Olympiad, Rome 1960', Cassell, 1960

Richard Askwith, 'The Rise and Fall of Emil Zatopek, Olympic Legend', Yellow Jersey Press, 2016

Dick Booth, 'The Impossible Hero: A Life of Gordon Pirie', Corsica Press, 1999

Rick Broadbent, 'Endurance: The Extraordinary Life and Times of Emil Zatopek', John Wisden and Co, 2016

John Bryant, 'The Marathon Makers', John Blake Publishing Ltd, 2008

John Bryant, '3: 59.4: The Quest to Break the 4 Minute Mile', Random House Group Ltd, 2004

D A Jamieson and K M Whitton, '50 years of Athletics: An Historical Record of the Scottish Amateur Athletic Association 1883-1933', Scottish Amateur Athletic Association, 1933

Tim Johnston and Donald Macgregor, 'His Own Man: The Biography of Otto Peltzer', Pitch Publishing, 2016

John Keddie, 'Scottish Athletics 1883-1983: The Official Centenary Publication of the Scottish Amateur Athletic Association', Scottish Amateur Athletic Association, 1982

Donald Macgregor, 'Running My Life', Pinetree Press, 2010

Fergus Murray Training Diaries: 1960 to 1975 (unpublished)

Colin A. Shields, 'Runs Will Take Place Whatever the Weather: The Centenary History of the Scottish Cross Country Union 1890-1990', Scottish Cross Country Union, 1990

Scottish Athletics Yearbooks 1962 to 1975

Frank Stampfl, 'Running', Four Square Books, 1960

Periodicals:

Athletics Weekly: July 1960 to December 1975

Websites:

Edinburgh University Hare and Hounds

The Scottish Association of Track Statisticians

Scottish Athletics: Road Running and Cross Country Commission: The Archive

Scottish Distance Running History – Brian McAusland and Colin Youngson

Wikipedia

INDEX

126